1981

# Humanistic Culture Learning:
# An Introduction

# Humanistic Culture Learning: An Introduction

JOHN E. WALSH

An East-West Center Book 王
From the East-West Culture Learning Institute

Published for the East-West Center
by The University Press of Hawaii

**Library of Congress Cataloging in Publication Data**

Walsh, John E.
  Humanistic culture learning.

  Includes bibliographical references.
  1. Intercultural education.  I.  Title.
LC1099.W34       301.2'07          78-26859
ISBN 0-8248-0637-9

To my mother,
Jettie B. Walsh

# Contents

# Preface

This book intends simply to introduce those who, for whatever reason, are caught up in the need or the desire to learn another culture to one approach to *culture learning*. The only prerequisite for reading it is a stirring of interest in the people of another culture and an openness to the thought that there might be something exciting and rewarding in encountering and learning what these people think and why they behave as they do. Culture learning is still in an early stage of development as a field of study, but it can be expected to grow rapidly as the world in general becomes more interdependent and more internationalized. Many of us in the field of culture learning still feel somewhat like the man newly appointed to a high political office. When asked what he knew about his new position, he replied, "I know something more than absolutely nothing but much less than a little."

*Humanistic Culture Learning: An Introduction* has gone through a number of drafts in the several years since it was first conceived. The need for such a book, which is no less great now than it was then, first became clear to me during a semester-long seminar in 1972 at the East-West Center. An interdisciplinary team of anthropologists, sociologists, linguists, philosophers, and educators had been invited to the Center to: (1) explore the concept of culture learning, and (2) suggest directions that the then newly created Culture Learning Institute might take in helping to ameliorate the problems of misunderstanding in cross-cultural relationships.

The assignment was intriguing and, as an interdisciplinary effort, the seminar was excellent. Gregory Bateson, for one, seemed to me to be profoundly at home in all the disciplines represented as well as in several that were not. All the participants had been and were deeply involved in culture learning. Nonetheless, I had the feeling that all too often we were discussing *cultures* as if they were things or objects, when in reality they are peoples. As well, that we were discussing *culture learning* as if it were exclusively a scientific pursuit and not, equally important, a humane or humanistic interaction!

The seminar was most enlightening, and I am grateful for both the ideas and the friendships that emerged. This book, however, is in no way a report on or a summary of that seminar. Over the intervening years, my ideas of humanistic culture learning have been extended and clarified through numerous discussions with colleagues and students at the East-West Culture Learning Institute. I would like herewith to express my appreciation.

What do I mean by *humanistic culture learning*? Nothing more esoteric than that culture learning is a study *of* the group life of human beings *by* other human beings. When we study a culture, we confront a *Thou* or a *You* rather than an *It*, a thing, or an object. There is no such thing as culture in the abstract, apart from the people who embody it and live it, just as there is no freedom, love, or justice apart from the people who are or are not free, loving, and just. A culture, to be sure, is a collective or community *You*, but the culture learner can comprehend the culture only through individual human beings who express that culture in what they think and in how they behave.

Humanistic culture learning takes place as an act of the whole person, not just as an act of the learner's mind. And since culture learning is a *two-way interaction*, rather than a *one-way action*, the quality of the personal or human feelings involved make a big difference in what is or can be learned.

Humanistic culture learning is also based on the high probability that human beings of different cultures may have much to *learn from* other human beings as well as much *about them*. In this respect, humanistic culture learning is neither unscientific nor antiscientific; it welcomes any and all sources of scientific information. It posits simply that scientific method alone is inadequate to the task of establishing the mutual trust and respect, the deeper feelings and sensitivities, the intersubjectivity, and the connaturality or fellow feeling that go into *culture learning*. Intuition, insight, empathy, "vibrations," poetry, impressions, and feelings may be even more telling and more significant in culture learning than harder and more objective kinds of data.

Only after the final manuscript of this book had been completed did I have the opportunity to read Edward T. Hall's brilliantly insightful *Beyond Culture*. It was gratifying to discover that the central thesis of Hall's book and of this one are similar, namely, that culture learning is a first and indispensable step in a human's liberation from the narrow confinement of his or her own culture in the search for a higher community of mankind. Because this thesis is so basic and so urgent in the modern world, it is no surprise that it would be presented to the public in these two—and hopefully many more—books. Neither is it surprising that two authors should have approached this thesis in two entirely different ways.

Chapter 1 studies the new role and the greatly increased emphasis on culture learning in the modern world, and chapter 2 seeks to make clear what culture learning essentially *is*. Chapters 3, 4, 5, 6, and 7 examine respectively history, language, world views, law, and the arts as major humanistic modes of culture learning. The aim is to give the reader a general overview of how these modes of culture learning function in the learning of any particular culture. Chapter 8 considers how it is that culture learning leads beyond the learning of another culture and opens up the possibility of human community.

# Acknowledgments

The typing, retyping, and typing yet again of major and minor portions of this book was a shared effort of the clerical and secretarial staff of the Culture Learning Institute. I acknowledge with gratitude this continuing and good-spirited cooperation. Similarly, my colleagues and students at the East-West Culture Learning Institute will recognize how much they have influenced my thinking. I thank them for the sometimes pointed and sometimes subtle ways they have helped to make this a better book.

Carol Maeda, student assistant, deserves special mention for her diligence in tracing down references and checking sources.

# chapter 1

# Culture Learning for Tomorrow's World

Even before beginning our consideration of what culture learning is and how it proceeds, we need to explore the question of why anyone should be interested in culture learning in the first place. It is not self-evident that learning about another culture or other cultures should be included in school and college curriculums and regarded as one of the marks of a fully educated person in the modern world. A case might be made that people have a natural curiosity about how the people of other cultures think, feel, believe, value, and behave. But even if such a natural curiosity exists, most people are so preoccupied with what is close by and what comes daily within the orbit of their primary concerns that their curiosity is not often aroused. The historical record is fairly clear on the point that most people of most cultures have been inclined to live within their own cultures and have preferred the company of those of their own to the company of those outside their culture. Such things as walled cities, iron curtains, restrictions on travel and communication, laws against emigration and immigration, and prohibitions against "mixed marriages" are not modern inventions by any means.

There have always been exceptions, to be sure. Among the Greeks of classical times, for example, certain persons were sent out to other lands and cultures to see how other people lived and did things as a way of gaining ideas for the improvement of life back home. (These persons were called *thereroi* or "seers," from which the English word *theory* is derived.) Dealers in foreign trade and commerce, as well as those in diplomatic service, were generally expected to know the ways and cultural backgrounds of those foreigners with whom they came in contact. Religious missionaries would frequently learn the language and culture of the country in which they did their proselytzing, although their aim in doing so was often enough to bring about basic changes in those very cultures. Military conquests and occupations necessitated certain forms of culture learning, and sometimes cultural forces were such that the vanquished triumphed culturally over their military conquerors. Anthropologists and ethnographers have made particular cultures the objects of their intensive specialized study, and travellers and explorers have written accounts of the peoples with whom they resided or sojourned for longer or shorter periods of time. And, finally, every century has seen both refugees who were forced to become learners of another culture in order to survive and emigrants who took up life in another culture because they preferred that culture's ways and values to those of the culture in which they were born.

But overall, the number of those interested in other cultures has been very small in comparison with the total population of any given culture. It is estimated that, even in a country as mobile as the United States, less than 10 percent of the people have ever been outside their own country and only 1 percent have resided outside the country for any substantial amount of time.[1] What knowledge most Americans have of cultures other than their own would have been derived only from fragmented and peripheral studies in schools and colleges, or from casual reading and the mass media. The serious study of other cultures has been reserved for a limited number of advanced undergraduates and for specialists in specific geographical regions, generally called "area studies." Even when the study of a foreign language is undertaken in the schools, either on a voluntary or a required basis, the emphasis is most often on drill in the language itself rather than on the culture of which the language is a part.

Why is it, then, that culture learning has come to be seen, by growing numbers of educators and statesman alike, as a modern imperative and an essential ingredient in the shaping of the human thought and sentiment necessary for tomorrow's world?[2] Why is it that *cultural literacy,* understanding the opinions and behaviors of other people, is coming to be regarded as of equal importance with *functional literacy,* the basic ability to read and write or to communicate with verbal or mathematical language? This question could be answered in a number of ways, but they would all relate to the basic changes that have made the world a different kind of place than it ever was before. It is no longer realistic or practicable for any country or culture to think that even its own self-interests can best be served by isolating itself from the rest of the human community. The desire for political independence and self-government and the search for cultural identity have taken on new potency, but the stage on which human interactions take place is now as much global as local.

The point that the world has now become so small—at least from the viewpoint of modern science and technology—that it must be seen as planetary and interdependent has been made in so many ways and so many places that it need not be elaborated here.[3] Even ordinary laypeople, who are not well informed about lasers and masers, intercontinental missiles and thermonuclear weapons, automation and cybernation, artificial satellites and the mining of ocean beds, are aware of the impact of supersonic speed in today's transportation and the changes brought about by the possibility of instantaneous communication around the world. They have sensed the meaning of the term "global village" in watching television and movies, in reading the papers, and in listening to radio even in otherwise remote areas of the world. They are more or less keenly aware that recessions and inflations are not limited to any one culture or country and that pollution of the air and the oceans can affect human beings everywhere.

Culture learning has been made essential and urgent simply by reason of the nature of the new world in which we now live and in which our children will be living in the future. Put in the bluntest terms possible, culture learning is the best, if not the only, means available to us for coming to grips with the fact that the earth's three and a half billion human inhabitants must find a way of living together harmoniously and humanely on a very small planet. If no man is an island, it is equally true that no culture or country, whether large or small, can any longer be an island, cut off from contact or interaction with other cultures and thinking of its ecosphere and biosphere as belonging to itself alone. Culture learning is the crucial step, the vitally necessary breakthrough in the developing of what Julian Huxley, as Director General of the United Nations Educational, Scientific, and Cultural Organization (UNESCO), called a "world philosophy, a unified and unifying background of thought for the modern world."[4] The general welfare of the human race—and perhaps its very survival—depends on the emergence of such a unifying background of thought. The first stage in developing this world philosophy might be to find common grounds and reasons sufficiently strong to win the assent of all nations to the nonviolent resolution of their conflicts, in the realization that a third World War might well mean the extinction of the human species. But the concept of a unified and unifying background of thought goes far beyond this in the direction of striving to find the bases and the methods for human cooperation and the building of human community.

Since the foregoing is the basic thesis of this book and since at first glance it might seem to be claiming too much for culture learning—or placing too great a burden upon it—further clarification is necessary along at least two lines: (1) the phenomenon of culture itself, and (2) the relation of diverse cultures to an overarching world community or to the emergence of a unifying world philosophy.

## The Phenomenon of Culture

We will be considering a definition of *culture* a little later, but for now we are concerned simply with what might be called the phenomenology of culture. One most evident and inescapable starting point is that every human being is born into a particular culture, that is, every baby is born at some time and in some place and has a particular set of parents. Whether the biological parents themselves, surrogate parents, relatives, or the State will be responsible for the child's health and education is itself a matter of cultural determination. Whoever "rears" the child will have definite ideas, which they have learned in turn from their observations and experiences within the culture, of how the child should be brought up. The culture's ways of doing, seeing, saying, and evaluating things will inevitably become the child's ways because this is the only world he at first knows. If the newly born happens to be the child of a culture in which outlooks and attitudes are rapidly changing, its induction into the culture is likely to be less certain, planned, formal, rigid, and prescribed than if it were born into a more static and traditional society. But even in rapidly changing cultures, the child soon learns that within its culture some central things are relatively more permanent and abiding than others. Culture is a universal phenomenon in that no one is born "cultureless," that is, no one is born free of other people who have more or less fixed and definite ideas of how children should be brought up and what they should think and value.

A second phenomenon connected with the concept of culture besides its inevitability is that it can be seen as serving a very useful social and psychological purpose. A group's culture gives that group or society its cohesiveness, solidarity, identity, and security. The child, on being born into the culture, soon learns its language, its myths and symbols, its ways of classifying, categorizing, and punctuating reality, and its ways of assigning roles and rewards and punishments. Largely subconsciously, the child accepts the culture as his or her own, as the tradition out of which he sprang, as where he belongs and feels at home. It is the culture which, according to a very powerful way of expressing the idea, "mediates" the world to the individual. Without such mediation, each child would have to start from the beginning on his own to find sense or to make sense out of what otherwise would be nothing less than the chaos of everyday experiencing. This phenomenon is perhaps best summarized, in the term given to it by Peter L. Berger and Thomas Luckmann, as "universe-maintenance."[5]

A third phenomenon, closely connected with the culture principle, is the tendency of those who are part of any culture to assume that their particular culture is right, best, "reality oriented," or in accord with nature and common sense in its ways of doing and seeing things. This tendency itself is variable in intensity from culture to culture, but that it exists in most if not all cultures is beyond dispute. Those living within a culture that has little contact with other cultures tend to view their culture's ways of thinking, doing, and valuing both as the best way and as the only normal and natural way. Even those persons who come more or less regularly into contact with people of other cultures, not as potential learners but as potential teachers, will tend to think that "our way" is better, more reasonable and more logical, more convenient and practical, more ancient, more hygienic, more aesthetically pleasing, more human, more divinely inspired than "their way." Such persons will find good explanations for why—to use a somewhat superficial example—it is "better" to use a knife and fork than chopsticks or vice versa. Or, as a much more serious example, they will find it silly, if not threatening, that some people should regard the cow as sacred when common sense dictates that if there are any sacred animals at all they are really the elephant or the monkey. In short, cultures tend to look with fear and hostility on any ideas that might undermine the validity, authenticity, and legitimacy of their own ideas.

Finally, at least with reference to the major phenomenon of culture, both the historical facts and philosophical analysis seem to indicate that there always has been and always will be a multiplicity of cultures. Assuming that human beings are free, creative, curious, and intelligent, it is most unlikely that any one set of ideas, values, or behaviors would ever become so compelling that all people everywhere would come to accept them. Historians such as Toynbee and Spengler have written voluminously about the rise and fall of various major cultures and civilizations throughout men's history. William Hickling Prescott, the distinguished American historian, wrote brilliant accounts of the Inca and Aztec cultures that are of special historical interest because they reveal so graphically how high civilizations sometimes disappear all together, except for the archeological artifacts they may have left behind. As we shall see later, there is an important difference between a *culture* and a *nation,* but one indication of the number of cultures in today's world is the fact that there are some hundred and seventy-five nations and dependencies, each making claim to some kind of distinctive cultural identity.

Philosophers have disputed the question of whether or not

there is any such thing as "human nature," since at least the time of Aristotle and Plato. If it could be shown that there is something substantive rather than purely functional or nominal in the concept of human nature, then it might be held that the purpose of all groups or societies would be to make it possible for individuals to come as close as possible to the achieving or perfecting of their human nature. It would imply that there is one objectively best way of becoming human or being human. Cultures would be good or bad, right or wrong, vital or disintegrating depending on their capacity for opening up the possibility for man to live in accord with his real, true, and objective nature. Ultimately, the question of whether or not there is such as thing as human nature is metaphysical. This very question, as would be expected if the concept of culture is valid, will be answered differently in different cultures. Christians, for example, are likely to hold to an interpretation much different from that of Buddhists or Hindus.

Berger and Luckmann, writing on this subject from a sociological perspective, state: "While it is possible to say that man has a nature, it is more significant to say that man constructs his own nature, or more simply that man produces himself."[6] They further suggest that "it is an ethnological commonplace that the ways of becoming and being human are as numerous as man's cultures," and that:

> In other words, the process of becoming man takes place in an interrelationship with an environment. This statement gains significance if one reflects that this environment is both a natural and a human one. That is, the developing human being not only interrelates with a particular natural environment, but with a specific cultural and social order, which is mediated to him by significant others who have charge of him . . . . From the moment of birth, man's organismic development, and indeed a large part of his biological being as such, are subjected to continuing socially determined interference.[7]

Since any culture is the result of interrelationships and interactions between a natural environment and a human one, it will surprise no one to find that there are many different cultures in the world. There are, in fact, many different natural environments and many different ways in which human beings can interact with each other and with their natural environment. People living in a naturally fertile tropical environment, to take an obvious example, have different kinds of interrelationships with that environment than do people living in a less fertile environment. One interesting illustration of this point is the theory that Judaism, Christianity, and Islam, all monotheistic religions, originated in a desert environment and that their monotheism is traceable in part to the central presence and role of the sun in man's life in a desert environment. That physical or natural environment is only an influencing and not a determining factor in the forming of cultures, however, is well evidenced by the fact that groups living in roughly comparable natural environments will not infrequently have greatly different cultures.

In the same way, people living in one kind of human environment will also have different kinds of interrelationships with that environment than those living in other kinds of human environments. For just one example, people living in a human environment in which literacy is stressed and valued will have interrelationships with that environment is stressed and valued will have interrelationships with that environment different from those in which literacy is not emphasized. John S. Mbiti, former professor at Makerere University in Uganda, points out:

> Only a few of the people of Africa had written scripts of their own before writing was introduced to them by Christian missionaries in the nineteenth and twentieth centuries. The literacy rate is as low as 5% in some countries today. Communication continues to be carried on largely through oral tradition, rituals, drama, art, symbols, and ceremonies. These are the means by which the history, customs, skills, literature, religion, and philosophy of the African peoples have been preserved and handed on from one generation to another.[8]

In terms of literacy and all that it implies, African culture will then be considerably different from, for example, the Japanese or American cultures, in which such high value is placed on literacy that it is simply taken for granted that everyone will be able to read and write.

The important point for the moment is that cultures are constructed by people interacting with their environments. Their way of interacting with these environments are numerous; there

is no one predetermined "real" or human way in which these interrelationships must or should take place. Cultures are formed
and maintained by people seeing, sensing, or feeling that their
way of doing things and explaining things supplies them with
sufficient purpose, satisfaction, order, and security to make life
bearable and hopefully fulfilling and enjoyable.

## The Relationships of Individual Cultures to an Overarching World Culture

We have seen, then, that cultures are inevitable in that no one
can be "cultureless" or "culture-free," that they serve an important social psychological function, that they tend to maintain and
legitimate themselves through various reality and identity tests,
and that even on a planet as small as Earth, there are many kinds
of natural and human environments that give rise to a plurality
and diversity of culture. Do not these very phenomena which
tend to guarantee and perpetuate the fact of cultural differences
elevate culture to a kind of ultimate, thus making the emergence
of any viable world culture or world community not only impossible but inconceivable? Mankind is faced with the extremely difficult task of making sure the answer to that question is no.

The problem of how to develop a unifying world philosophy
out of a large number of discrete cultures, each with its own
ideas and values, its own interests and intense loyalties, is by no
means a new problem. It is in fact a very old problem that takes
on only a new special and dramatic meaning in the modern
world. Reinhold Niebuhr, looking out upon the world as World
War II was coming to an end, wrote correctly and convincingly
that the problem of overcoming international chaos and of
extending the principle of community to worldwide terms has
become the most urgent of all the issues which face our epoch.[9]

Niebuhr went on to speak of the two forces tending toward
some kind of world philosophy or world community: the one,
the older force, derived from a sense of moral obligation which
transcends the geographical and other limits of specific cultures,
and the other, the newer force, tending toward world community
that derives from the global interdependence of nations and
culture brought about by the advances of technology.[10]

The concept of an overarching world or human community

made up of disparate cultures implies cooperation *among* individual specific cultures rather than the disappearance of cultural differences and diversities. Community does not mean a completely standardized and homogenized way of looking at things and doing things throughout the world. Even if such unanimity were possible, it would make the world a far duller and less interesting place in which to live. But people coming together freely and openly in the forming of individual cultures will inevitably structure or construct those ways of living in accordance with their differing perceptions of what is real, valid, and important for them. Advances in technology, to be sure, tend to carry with them a powerful standardizing dynamic, but even technology itself and the values placed on it vary from culture to culture. And technology, by decreasing the amount of time and effort that human beings must devote to survival, can make it possible for cultures to develop their own identities in their own individual ways in those areas of life in which technology plays a much lesser role, if any at all—that is, for example, in religion, philosophy, and the arts, and in the quality of personal and social relationships. The violent or forceful imposing of an ideology by one culture on another is the exact antithesis of community.

Neither does the concept of a world or human community necessarily suggest some form of world government. This might or might not result from a world community in which the peoples of the world felt they were genuinely sharing and participating and from which they were benefiting, but it is not at all essential to the basic concept of world community. There is a popular tendency to equate a culture with a political or geographical community, so that being a member of the community also involves identity as a *citizen* of that community. In a parallel way, it is sometimes held that a world community would depend on the widespread feeling among people that they are *world citizens*, under a world government. But is it possible, for example, for a person to identify with the Christian community or the Buddhist community without being a citizen of any particular nation state? Nonetheless, world community does imply that the people of the world had arrived at some working consensus on the rule of law, rather than the rule of force. Individual persons would be participants, *citizens,* in the sense that they felt responsible for living in accordance with a rule of law.

There are those who think that the very idea of a world culture or world community is inherently contradictory, that is, that human beings can identify only with smaller, primary, face-to-face groups and that the group of "all human beings" is just too large and diverse to be meaningful. The idea is rejected out of hand as utopian and hopelessly idealistic. John Adams, writing at the time of the founding of the American republic, spoke for a long tradition of realist thinkers before and since his time when he stated: "I have long been settled in my opinion that neither philosophy, nor religion, nor morality, nor wisdom, nor interest, will ever govern nations or parties, against their vanity, pride, resentment or revenge, or their avarice or ambition. Nothing but force and power and strength can restrain them."[11] The historical record of man's inhumanity to man would seem to come down heavily in support of Adam's position.

Yet there is a correspondingly long line of thinkers and educators who take a much different point of view, namely, that a world culture is not only not an inherently contradictory concept but also that its realization is well within man's powers and hopes. Among the most eloquent spokesmen for this point of view is Karl Jaspers. He writes: "But who is man, who knows himself bound to nation, race, sex, epoch, sphere of culture, social and economic situation, and yet can break free, place himself as it were outside and above all these things in which he is historically immersed?"[12] And out of an altogether different cultural tradition, Rabindranath Tagore writes that: "The inmost creed in India is to find the one in the many, unity in diversity. India does not admit difference to be conflict, nor does she espy an enemy in every stranger. So she repels none, destroys none, and strives to find a place for all in a vast social order. She acknowledges every path and recognizes greatness wherever she finds it."[13] The basic relationship of the world cultures to a world culture is, indeed, that of the one and the many—or even better *the one in the many*—of unity in diversity—and it is that which must now be considered.

A world culture or world community might be viewed

theoretically either as a set of definite ideas and values which the people of the world might share and hold in common or as a set of processes which simply make it possible for the increasing number of world problems that spill over cultural or national boundaries to be attended to with a minimum of friction and a maximum of fairness to all involved. These two possibilities overlap in many ways. Consensus on a way of resolving problems or a process for resolving conflicts, for example, is in itself of high value. Either construct would imply that the defining of the single world culture had been arrived at by the free—rather than the forced—consent of all those who were members of the global culture. And either construct would imply that one way out of the many possible alternative ways had been selected as the basis for decision making and practical action.

Although the main emphasis here is on the vital importance of the emergence of a world culture or world community rather than on trying to outline, describe, or define what that culture would be, a further word about the two models of a world culture just suggested might be helpful. The first model stresses substance; the second stresses process.

The first suggests finding and clarifying what it is that the cultures of the world, now standing as it were "alongside" one another, actually do have or could have in common. This might be called a "common denominator" view of world culture. Those who hold this view insist that, in spite of their many and profound differences, the peoples of the world already have much more in common than they are aware of. World culture would simply stress the common bonds and the unifying elements. It would emerge organically while educational systems, as a major part of the enterprise, would be revamped to emphasize commonalities rather than differences. Julian Huxley, for example, thinks that such a common denominator might be found in humanism. Huxley's own humanism had a strongly scientific bent; his ideas have encountered much opposition, but they are a remarkably lucid statement of an attempt to find a common denominator. Huxley writes:

> . . . humanism must clearly be a world humanism, both in the sense of seeking to bring in all the peoples of the world, and of treating all

peoples and individuals within each people as equals in terms of human dignity, mutual respect, and educational opportunity. It must also be a scientific humanism, in the sense that the application of science provides most of the material basis for human culture, and also that the practice and the understanding of science need to be integrated with that of the other human activities. It cannot, however, be materialistic, but must embrace the spiritual and mental as well as the material aspects of existence, and must attempt to do so on a truly monistic, unitary philosophic basis.[14]

The United Nations Universal Declaration of Human Rights would be a different example of a substantive or common denominator grounds for developing a world culture. All signatories to the Declaration indicated their consensus on what were and what were not human rights.

The second model of a world culture consists not so much in a consensus on the substance of ideas and values but on ways of getting things done. It would be a consensus, not on any theological, philosophical, legal, social, or economic system, but on how to conduct the business of the world in such a way as to promote the good of all and the greatest good of the greatest number. It is conceivable that people the world over could agree to cooperate and work together for specific purposes—for example, in a drastic reduction in the amount now spent on arms or an all-out effort to increase the world's food supply—without concurring in any particular rationale for the action to be taken. As mentioned earlier, however, the distinction between substance and process is not a complete or exclusive one. In the example just given, agreement on the need for cooperative efforts for increasing food supplies is already an agreement on substantive ideas and values.

The main thesis may now be restated in this way: The central and most compelling task of our time is to work toward the emergence of a unified and integrated overarching human culture in a world made up of many diverse and often contradictory particular cultures. To make progress toward the achieving of this all-important goal, culture learning needs to be better understood, greatly improved, and made much more available to people throughout the world. It is through *culture learning* and through culture learning alone that one comes to grasp the meaning, value, and significance in daily life of the cultural concept itself—that is, how the culture shapes the mentalities of those who belong to it. It is also by means of culture learning that one comes to acquire, at one and the same time, both a commitment to one's own culture and the detachment from it necessary to make participating in a world culture possible, intelligible, and vividly real. *Culture learning* may well be considered an end or a goal in itself—just as knowledge of any kind can be considered a good or a value in itself on the assumption that knowledge makes for a better and fuller human existence—but in the modern interdependent world, culture learning also has a newer expanded role and a deeper mission, namely, aiding in the emergence of a world community.

Emory S. Bogardus sees the relationship between individual cultures and an overarching world culture or community as basically one of point of view. Culture learning makes possible the recognition of broader vistas. People are no less members of their own cultures or nations by reason of the fact that they also actively share in a more extensive world culture. He writes:

> World community includes both a world idea and a community idea blended into one. The world aspect includes all the peoples and the community aspect, a set of social relationships. Together, world community involves a point of view, a way of looking at human problems that supplements, but does not supplant, an individual viewpoint, a family viewpoint, a local viewpoint, a national viewpoint.[15]

And Margaret Mead sees the relationship between individual cultures and world culture in a more functional way, as the recognizing of similarities between one's own culture and that of other persons. She states: "In general, the more the people of the world recognize *certain* symbols, values, and purposes as both their own and those of all the other peoples of the world, and give to those symbols, values, and purposes a high place, the more the world is a community."[16]

It is in culture learning, to which we next turn, that our viewpoints are expanded and broadened, our recognition of the similarities as well as the differences among cultures is sharpened, and our feelings about the possibility of the emergence of a true world community are reinforced.

NOTES

1. The number of Americans travelling abroad, exclusive of military personnel, other government employees and their dependents, and U.S. citizens residing abroad, increased from just over a million in 1955 to approximately six and a half million in 1974, a large jump by any measure. Yet this is a small fraction of the 212 million people residing in the United States in 1974. *Statistical Abstract of the United States* (Washington, D.C.: U.S. Dept. of Commerce, Bureau of Census,1975), p. 219.

2. See, for example, "The Declaration of Interdependence" drafted by Henry Steele Commager as part of the World Affairs Council of Philadelphia's Bicentennial Era program. *Intellect* 105:2376 (July-August, 1976): 4–5.

3. See, for example, Herman Kahn and Anthony J. Wiemer, *The Year 2000* (London: The Macmillan Company, 1967). Also the references, notes and elaboration in Bruce C. Murray, *Navigating the Future* (New York: Harper & Row, 1975), pp. 158–173, contain an excellent brief bibliography.

4. Julian Huxley, *UNESCO: Its Purpose and Its Philosophy* (Washington, D.C.: Public Affairs Press, 1948), p. 46.

5. Peter L. Berger and Thomas Luckmann, *The Social Construction of Reality* (New York: Doubleday, 1966), p.96ff.

6. Ibid., p. 47.

7. Ibid., p.46.

8. John S. Mbiti, "The Forest Has Ears," *PHP*7:7 (July, 1976): 17.

9. Reinhold Niebuhr, *The Children of Light and the Children of Darkness* (New York: Charles Scribner's Sons, 1944), p.153.

10. Ibid., p. 154.

11. Quoted by John P. Diggans, Los Angeles Times Service, in "Politics Offers No Salvation," editorial in the Honolulu *Sunday Star-Bulletin & Advertiser,* June 20, 1976, p. B–3.

12. Karl Jaspers, *Philosophy Is for Everyone* trans. R. F. C. Hull and Grete Wels. (New York: Harcourt, Brace & World,1967), p. 34.

13. Rabindranath Tagore, *Towards Universal Man* (New York: Asia Publishing House, 1961), pp. 65–66.

14. Huxley, *UNESCO*, p. 5.

15. Henry S. Bogardus, *Toward a World Community* (Los Angeles: University of Southern California Press, 1964), iii.

16. Margaret Mead, "World Culture" in *The World Community,* ed. Quincy Wright (Chicago: University of Chicago Press, 1948), p. 47.

*chapter* 2
# What Is Culture Learning?

What, then, is culture learning? In this chapter we will consider culture learning in itself; subsequent chapters will examine individually several of the more specific and basic modes or means of culture learning.

First, what is culture, or better, what is *a culture?* It is a commonplace in introductions to the concept of culture to point out that there are almost as many definitions of the word "culture" as there are people who use the word. Anthropologists employ the term in a very broad sense to include everything, material or mental, that is characteristic of any given society and distinguishes it from other societies. The word "culture" is sometimes capitalized when it is meant to denote a society's best material and mental achievements and uncapitalized when it is used to denote the whole complex of material and mental characteristics. This is needlessly complicated. It would be difficult to improve on Ralph Linton's simple definition of culture as the "way of life of any society."[1] Linton goes on briefly to explain: "This way of life includes innumerable details of behavior but all of these have certain factors in common. They all represent the normal, anticipated response of any of the society's members to a particular situation . . . . Such a consensus of behavior and opinion constitutes a culture pattern; the culture as a whole is a more or less organized aggregate of such patterns."[2] When the word "culture" is used in this book, it means a "consensus of behavior and opinion" so aggregated or institutionalized as to constitute a "way of life." The controlling word here is "consensus"; where there is no consensus, there is no culture.

The Oxford English Dictionary indicates that the word *consensus* comes from two Latin words: *con*, meaning together or with, and *sentire*, meaning to feel, think, judge. The English word "consensus" thus means to think, feel, or judge together and thus to agree. When people have come to think, feel, judge in the same way—when they agree—they have formed a consensus, a culture. Put negatively, one culture differs from another in that the people of culture A do not have the same thoughts and behaviors as the people of culture B. Not only do the people of one culture not have the same cognitive and behavior patterns as the people of another culture, they also do not have the same experiences out of which consensus might grow. The people of culture A have their own consensuses, but these are not the same consensuses as those in culture B.

A word must be inserted here about the nature of the group experiences that form and shape the consensuses within a culture. Although human beings are flexible, adaptable, and creative, the range of their possible experiences is not unlimited. Human beings, to give one simple example, cannot survive without eating and drinking, and cultures cannot survive without procreating. All cultures will, therefore, inevitably share certain common experiences. But cultures differ vastly in the way they express, interpret, value, and legitimatize even the common experiences. All cultures, for example, experience the need for smooth and harmonious interpersonal relationships, but some give much greater priority and prominence to these relationships than other cultures do.

The word "consensus" is most illuminating in that it implies group agreement or commonality in opinion and behavior. It denotes collective and general opinion and behavior patterns, but it does not necessarily denote complete unanimity. The word "consensus" also helps us to avoid the rather trivial question that is sometimes asked: How many people does it take to make a culture? Hypothetically, two people on an isolated island could form a culture; ordinarily, however, when we use the word "culture," we are talking about larger, but indefinite, numbers of people. To say, for example, that there is a consensus in America about the values of freedom would not necessarily mean that every individual American puts a high value on freedom, only that the people generally do. "Consensus," then, is as much an analytic term as it is a quantitative one. A vote or a public opinion poll is one way of determining whether a consensus is present in a society, but there are also other equally valid ways.

A culture thus exists wherever there is a sufficient consensus on opinion and behavior to give the group solidarity, cohesiveness, and identity. Within any larger human grouping or society, there may be, and usually are, persons who come together in a consensus on particular opinions or behaviors that are generally compatible or congruent with the culture's essential or principal consensuses but which also deviate from it more or less strongly. Such consensuses, as those found among minority groups of age, race, religion, or vocation, are classified as subcultures. There are also very likely to be in any society some persons who agree among themselves that the fundamental premises or principles of the overall culture of which they are presently members need to be changed. These types of consensuses are classified as *countercultures;* on a political spectrum they may exist either far to the right or far to the left of the mainstream consensuses.

It is vital, in attempting to understand the concept of culture, to distinguish between a culture and a nation and between culture and race.

The first distinction is a little more difficult to grasp because of the all too frequent practice, usually as a matter of convenience, of identifying a culture with a particular country or nation. One frequently hears, for example, of Mexican culture, American culture, New Zealand culture, or Indonesian culture, as if each country had its own culture or as if culture and nation were coterminus concepts. In fact, however, a country or a nation is a political and geographical, not a cultural, unit. The same basic culture, the same basic consensuses, may prevail in a number of different countries or nations, and conversely a number of cultures may exist in the same country or political unit. One thinks immediately, for example, of the Muslim culture that so strongly determines the "way of life" in a number of countries not only in the Middle East but elsewhere. And one thinks of the number of different cultures and languages in a single country such as Papua New Guinea.

The second distinction, that between culture and race, is more clear-cut and, in the modern world, more crucial, since racism is still so virulent and inimical to harmonious human relationships. The essence of the distinction is that culture is *learned* or acquired and that race is *genetic* or inherited. The custom of dividing mankind into races according to skin color has served no good purpose socially or politically, and is of highly dubious scientific validity. Rather, it has served to set race against race and to inhibit the growth of the feeling that all persons belong to one race—the human race. The distinction between culture and race, important as it is, need not long detain us here. Attention must be called, however, to the work of Nathan Glazer and others who question whether the differences among groups can be explained purely on cultural grounds. Glazer claims that anthropologists who maintained that differences among groups are not genetic but cultural, that is, based on the transmission of custom, practices, values, and ideals rather than genes, are motivated by a desire to make people more tolerant of those group differences. He concedes that if people can be convinced they are not fated biologically to be what they are, group characteristics can change rapidly as environment, incentives, and policy change. But he also argues that we do not know yet what the relationship between heredity and environment is. He adds: "But at least the matter is sufficiently complicated to require a very long time indeed before we can move from what we know about human heredity and its complex interaction with environment today to a conclusion as to what, if any, part of human differences in living societies can be attributed to heredity."[3]

Attention must also be called to the fact that Arnold Toynbee, writing as an historian and not as an anthropologist, arrived at much the same conclusion regarding race as the anthropologists Franz Boas and Ruth Benedict—the two mentioned specifically by Glazer. Toynbee writes:

I reject all pretensions to spiritual superiority on the score of physical race, whatever may be the human breed on whose behalf these pretensions are being put forward. I do not know of there being any evidence for any correlation between physical and spiritual characteristics. The pretension is, I believe, as unscientific as it certainly is offensive.[4]

A further way of distinguishing among cultures must be introduced at this point. It is the distinction between so-called vertical cultures and horizontal cultures. A vertical culture is a consensus or a way of life that embraces all people in a given country or region, from the youngest to the oldest, the richest to the poorest, the governed to the governors. Chinese culture or American culture would be examples of vertical cultures. A horizontal culture, on the other hand, is made up of people united in a consensus or way of life along special interests or class lines. The idea of horizontal culture owes its origin and strength to the class philosophy and the social and economic thought of Karl Marx.[5] In this sense, culture and class become virtually the same thing.

Marx wrote about how much the different classes—the poor, the peasants, the laboring classes, the bourgeoisie, and the landed rich—have in common with each other around the world. He stressed, for example, that the workers of one country or region have greater agreement, more in the nature of a consensus or way of life, with the workers of other regions than they do with the wealthy and landed in their own countries. The same would be true, according to Marx, for all the other classes. Each class has its own way of thinking and behaving depending on its economic status. When, at the end of the Communist Manifesto, Marx and Engels call on workingmen of all countries to unite, they are addressing what they consider to be a horizontal culture, that is, the culture of all workingmen everywhere. "The workingmen have no country."[6] Marx made much of the idea that it is not our consciousness that determines our experience but our experience that determines our consciousness. Since our consciousness is, for Marx, predominantly an economic consciousness, it is our class or economic consciousness that determines our ways of thinking and behaving, that is, our culture. (For an excellent treatment of consciousness and experience from a phenomenologist point of view that differs greatly with Marx's economic determinism, see Maurice Merleau-Ponty's now almost classic *The Primacy of Perception and Other Essays.*[7])

A more contemporary example of the difference between vertical and horizontal cultures—and one that is frequently used for analytical purposes—is the distinction between urban and rural cultures. People living in large cities around the world might be said to have a culture of their own without regard to the countries (vertical cultures) in which they are located. Similarly, those living in rural areas, whether they be rich, poor, or middle class, may share important consensuses on opinion and behavior with others in rural areas without regard to political boundaries.

Keeping in mind the idea that a culture is simply a "consensus on opinion and behavior" is the key to clarifying the essential nature of *culture learning*. Fundamentally, culture learning can be nothing other than the learning of those consensuses on opinion and behavior that prevail in any group or society, the word "learning" for the moment being taken in the same way as we use it when we speak of learning anything else—for example, history, geography, philosophy, mathematics. Technically, then, the subject matter, or what is to be learned, in culture learning or culture study is the consensuses themselves that comprise and delineate the culture. There is thus no real difference in the basic meaning of culture learning whether one is learning the consensuses that prevail in one's own native culture or those that prevail in other cultures. The ways in which one's own culture is learned are, to be sure, considerably different from the ways in which other cultures are learned. For example, people do not deliberately and consciously set out to learn their own native culture; they learn their native culture, at least at first, simply by having been born in it, by being exposed to it, by *being* in it. Later on in life, culture learning of one's own culture may well become more formal and deliberate. Further, in culture learning as in all other kinds of learning there are an unlimited number of degrees of knowledge, ranging all the way from the most elementary to the most profound and sophisticated. The casual culture learner, a tourist, for example, or a beginning student, cannot ordinarily be credited with having achieved the same depth or degree of culture learning as a scholar who has made a particular culture the subject of his lifelong study.

While the learning of the consensuses that obtain in a culture might be called the objective of culture learning, the knowledge of these consensuses can reveal the culture only in its present form and as it now stands.

Consensuses, once established, tend to be both powerful and static. Culture learning, however, also involves coming to know the kinds and levels of dissent within the culture. This is so for at least two reasons: (1) dissent makes clear where the consensuses really are, how profoundly they are adhered to, and what measures are taken to protect them; and (2) dissent is dynamic in that it is concerned with cultural change and gives some indications of the directions in which the culture might be moving.

Understanding culture learning is, not unexpectedly, much more complex than would seem to be indicated in the preceding discussion. In an introduction to culture learning, it is not necessary to go into all these complexities or into any of them in great depth, but three further points are essential and require some elaboration.

First of all, the consensuses on opinion and behavior that form the object of culture learning or culture study are not something given in the physical material world or necessarily determined by it. These consensuses are ways in which different peoples have come to perceive and interpret their world and to respond to it and in it. First, a relatively simple example: If the people of one culture have come to a consensus on the opinion that chopsticks are more convenient, hygienic, and aesthetic than either fingers or forks, they will use chopsticks. In all probability, they could have developed other forms of "tools" to assist them in eating; indeed, it is highly likely they would have developed other forms if chopsticks did not serve their purposes well. This consensus on the use of chopsticks may change at some future time. In the meantime, however, chopsticks seem meaningful and satisfying to the people who use them, and these people are not likely to change easily their thinking that chopsticks are the normal, natural, and most effective way of transferring food to the human mouth.

The second example comes from a much deeper level of cultural functioning. If there is a consensus in a given culture on the opinion that "all men are created equal," this consensus will have arisen from a particular way in which the people of that culture view and respond to what they perceive to be the proper relationship among men, nature, and the Creator. Other cultures might well have a consensus to the effect that men were never intended to be regarded as equal with other men. And others might hold that ideas of equality might apply to men but not to women.

The point is that culture learning is a matter of the learner's coming to know a people's way of perceiving the world, that is, their consensuses on opinion and behavior. These consensuses on opinion and behavior are rarely such that they could not have been otherwise. Highly arbitrary, they represent the crystallization of that people's perception of how things are to be explained and done. In effect, then, culture learning consists of perceptions—the learner's perceptions of what the people of the particular culture perceive and of what has thus become living reality for them.[8] It would be unlikely that any two culture learners from the same culture would arrive at exactly the same conclusions, interpretations, or generalizations about a given culture. It would be even more unlikely that a culture learner from culture A and a learner from culture B would arrive at exactly the same conclusions about a third culture C. For example, a Japanese culture learner and an American one are likely to perceive quite different consensuses in Chinese culture. This means only that the subject matter of culture learning is not absolute objective eternal verity, but rather insights and illuminations that are more or less clarifying, significant, helpful in particular contexts and perspectives.

The second point, requiring further elaboration, concerns the nature of *learning* itself. Learning theory is one of the most widely disputed areas in contemporary psychology and it would take us too far afield to undertake even a sketchy survey of that question. It is sufficient here to emphasize that it is now well established that learning, or coming to know, is not simply a matter of intellect, important as that is. Learning something in the fullest sense also involves, among other things, a set of feelings toward what is to be learned that enters directly into the learning process. This feeling set, to be sure, is more evident and pronounced in some fields than in others. Feelings, positive or negative, greatly influence not only the quality of learning but even the capacity to learn. A person who is overly anxious or fearful, for example, at the thought of learning to play the piano will not be able to learn to play the piano—unless of course ways are found of overcoming such negative feelings. Similarly, negative or positive predispositions or feelings toward the people of a particular culture greatly influence learning that culture.

Learning anything, even learning to walk or talk, requires the necessary learning skills. At the higher levels these skills include memory, imagination, analysis, insight, attention or concentration, intuition, creativity, conceptualization, and generalization. Learning skills are necessary in the learning of one's culture, as well as in the learning of other cultures, even though much of the experiential learning of one's own culture takes place at the unconscious, pretheoretical, and precritical level.

It follows that the role of the teacher in culture learning, as in other forms of learning, is to facilitate the development of these learning skills in the learners. If one is to teach a particular culture, one must have first learned what the basic consensuses are within the culture to be taught. The teacher seeks to create the best possible learning environment, including the ordering and sequencing of the consensuses to be taught and learned, in such a way that the learners are aided in discovering for themselves the sources and the meanings of these consensuses.

People engage in learning something, whatever it may be, either so that they will simply understand the subject matter more fully or so that they will be able to do something with the knowledge they have gained. Culture learning is the same. One may well set out to learn another culture for no other reason than simply to know that culture. Learning or coming to know a culture, however, ordinarily implies more than just knowledge or cognitive apprehension. Even in the theoretical order, that is, the order of knowledge for its own sake, culture learning carries with it the implication of a search for the kind of knowledge that results in genuine understanding, respect, and appreciation. One need not agree with the consensuses discovered in other cultures, but one cannot be said to have learned another culture unless he understands how intelligent people could have arrived at these principles or consensuses—and unless he respects the honesty with which they are held.

In the more practical order, that is, doing something with what has been learned, the principal outcome of culture learning is the increased ability to *predict* how the people both of one's own and of other cultures will act and react in specific sets of circumstances. As a result of culture learning, one is in a better position to predict with a higher degree of accuracy, for example, what opinions and behavior patterns the people of a given culture will maintain at all costs—even the cost of life itself—and what opinions and behaviors will be more lightly held and easily changed. Like all knowledge, the knowledge acquired through culture learning is a form of power. And the power to predict or anticipate what the people of a given culture will think and do in practical circumstances or situations is an immense power that can be used either for worthy or for ignoble purposes. Cultural learning, practically considered, can and should serve as a basis for minimizing ethnocentrism and stereotypical thinking, and for maximizing tolerance, cooperation, and mutual understanding. But we must remember that culture learning can also result in knowledge which makes it possible for one culture to take advantage or exploit the people of another culture.

Culture learning, then, is not to be confused with intelligence gathering. The latter term usually implies the collecting of data or information which will be used, if possible and necessary, for such ulterior ends as national defense, expanded business opportunities, missionary efforts, and foreign aid policies. Intelligence gathering is not necessarily covert and can, when properly conducted, play an important part in culture learning. As Alfred North Whitehead pointed out, failing to get further information when such information would make a material difference in the quality of the decision is moral delinquency.

Humanistic culture learning, however, goes far beyond intelligence gathering. The very concept of humanistic culture learning implies mutuality and reciprocity, that is, that learning is taking place on both sides or on all sides. Those who simply gather intelligence are ordinarily not open to changes in their own thinking and behaving; they want to know what other

peoples are thinking and doing so that they can make more informed decisions about their possible actions and reactions. The
culture learner, on the contrary, is open to the possibility in the
process of culture learning that his own thought and feeling system might be strongly influenced and even completely changed.

The third point to be stressed here is that culture learning
takes two forms: developmental and deliberate. The child born
into a particular culture learns that culture, including its language, in a gradually unfolding and organic way. It is as natural
and effortless as growing up itself. Later, at some point, the
youth or adolescent may undergo some kind of an identity crisis
as he becomes more critical and more questioning of his own cultural principles, but most often even this identity crisis is resolved without great trauma as he comes to accept and affirm his
culture, both intellectually and emotionally.

The case of the young child who is born into one culture but
transferred very early in life to another culture is also a largely
developmental one. The child learns the second culture, starting
with its language, effortlessly, spontaneously, and with little or
no conscious reflection, discrimination, or judgment. In many
such cases the young child becomes both bilingual and bicultural
or even trilingual and tricultural without realizing that this is
something out of the ordinary. The child is literally as much at
home in one culture as another simply because he has grown up
in these cultures. Later in life, such a person may well undergo
intense emotional stress resulting from split loyalties and identities if forced to choose between or among the cultures in which
he has grown up. This might happen, for example, if he is forced
for legal reasons or for reasons of military service to declare one
country to be his country of citizenship.

On the other hand, culture learning can be—and often is—
deliberate. For any one or more of a number of good reasons, a
person sets out consciously and with deliberate choice to learn
another culture. He or she has the full intention of learning the
other culture and the full intention of taking all the means
necessary to achieve that goal. Since, as mentioned before,
culture learning is a matter of degree, this deliberate intention
may mean spending an entire lifetime in that effort. In certain
cases, culture learners go the full way, not only living in the

culture but also making the culture's basic cultural principles, its opinions and its behaviors, their own.

The distinction between *learning a culture* and *learning about a culture* becomes important at this point. This distinction can be helpful, but it can also be misleading.

*Learning a culture* often carries with it the connotation that one is in the process of learning a culture by means of living in that culture and experiencing it as fully as possible and at first hand. The implication is that, since a culture is a "way of life," learning a culture necessitates living that "way of life," immersing oneself in it. *Learning about a culture,* on the other hand, is often taken to be a somewhat inferior form of culture learning that implies learning a culture from the outside through secondary sources rather than through immediate experiencing and direct contact. In fact, however, living in a culture, even for an extended period of time, does not guarantee the learning of that culture. One has to want to learn the culture and seek actively to do so. On the other hand, one can learn a culture well through the organized and judicious use of secondary sources, including living teachers, interpreters, and informants. Most people would probably agree, however, that culture learning, ideally considered, would involve some measure of both living in the culture, that is, experiencing the culture, its language, and its people directly (learning the culture), and also studying such things as the culture's history (which cannot be experienced), its literature, its legal system, its philosophical principles, its technology, and its art forms through the best secondary sources available.

The formal culture teacher, whether the generalized instructor of the lower grades or the more specialized culture teacher at the advanced levels is, after all, a secondary source. So, however, is anyone of whom the culture learner might inquire if he were actually living in the culture. The primary source of culture learning, the learner's own direct observation and experience, may be valid and accurate but may also be distorted by reason of the culture learner's interests and background. On the other hand, knowledge gained from a well-qualified secondary source, an expert witness, may be just as valid as any gained through direct experience. The experience, for example, of actually living in a Japanese home is enormously different from seeing one in photographs or movies or from hearing a good lecture on Japanese home and family life. But the quality of knowledge and the depth of insight gained may be the same in the one as the other. In fact, seeing the movie or hearing the lecture may be better for culture learning purposes.

The culture learner or culture teacher must be aware of another important fact, namely, that a culture or the consensuses on opinion or behavior that make up a way of life is to a fairly large—but indeterminate—extent a matter of unconscious thought and behavior. Culture in this regard has frequently been compared to an iceberg, three fourths of which is invisible because it is below the surface of the ocean waters. Many if not most of the people within any culture think as they do and behave as they do most of the time simply because this is the way it is done. The particular way of seeing and doing things that prevails in the culture works well, or at least well enough so that it is not constantly called into question or raised to the conscious level. Culture learning, then, takes on the interesting characteristic of being frequently the articulation of assumptions, presuppositions, or premises that the people of the culture itself might not be able to identify or explain as well as an outside investigator can.

In this way culture learning might be likened to individual psychoanalysis. The skillful analyst may know more about persons undergoing analysis than the patients themselves know. In *Civilization and Its Discontents,* Sigmund Freud made the point that the development of a culture shows a far-reaching similarity to the development of an individual.[9] He illustrates the point particularly by indicating how whole cultures as well as individuals come to acquire a sense of guilt. What is important to note, however, is that the very things the culture learner seeks to discover are in large measure not in the consciousness but in the unconscious even of those who are members of that culture. Freud gives credit to Kant for showing us that our perceptions are subjectively conditioned and must not be regarded as identical with what is perceived but is in itself unknowable. He reminds us that, like the physical, the psychical is in reality not necessarily what it appears to us to be. This same idea is well expressed by John C. Condon, communications theorist, who writes that " . . . most communication is *not verbal,* is *not purposive,* and is *not within our self-conscious awareness.*"[10]

The distinction between the conscious and the unconscious elements in the forming and functioning of a culture could easily be confused with the equally important distinction between the *deep structure* and the *surface structure* of a culture. The distinction between deep structure and surface structure has an intellectual history that goes back at least as far as Plato's allegory of the cave in *The Republic.* The distinction is introduced here and explored more fully in chapter 4, "Culture Learning and Language Learning."

The culture, as such, does not have either a conscious or an unconscious, although Jung and others have seen some value in the concept of what is called the "collective unconscious." As applied to cultures, these terms are used analogously, with the individual human being as the primary analogue. Only individuals have a conscious and unconscious. Many of the ways of seeing and doing things in a culture are latent, outside of the present awareness, and taken for granted by the persons who comprise the culture. They are unexamined—perhaps even unexaminable—and in that sense unconscious. A person may be part of a consensus on the proposition that "all men are created equal" without being conscious of that consensus at all, at least until some challenge to the proposition forces it into his conscious awareness. Some consensuses on opinion and behavior are part of the unconscious in the sense that "everybody knows that," and in the sense that "we do it that way because everyone does it that way."

The distinction between the deep structure and the surface structure of a culture, however, is intended to help make clear a different set of ideas. The deep structure of a culture is the sum of those consensuses on opinions or behaviors that underlie or serve as an intellectual and emotional foundation for its collective life. They are essential to it, they form and integrate it to such a degree that if they change the culture it is no longer recognizable as the same culture. Thus, for example, the profit motive may be said to be in the deep structure of American culture because the profit motive underlies the American free enterprise system and because it determines such a large part of what

Americans think and how they behave. Without the profit motive, American culture would be an entirely different kind of culture—for better or for worse. No one would say that the profit motive is part of the unconscious in American life; it is rather very much in the consciousness of most Americans most of the time. The deep structure is made up, then, of those relatively unchanging basic opinions and behaviors, whether consciously or unconsciously accepted, that constitute the mainstay of a culture and give it its most important and meaningful cultural identity.

The surface structure, on the other hand, is that set of consensuses on opinion and behavior that are more apparent and more readily observable. The consensus in a culture on the proposition that authority and age should be respected would be considered part of the culture's deep structure, but such matters as who is introduced first, who eats first, and whose advice is sought most often would be surface manifestations of that consensus. Similarly, the consensus on the inviolability of contracts or on the need to keep one's promises would be part of a culture's deep structure that would be observable in the culture's surface structure in innumerable day-to-day transactions. The closer to the culture's surface a given consensus is, the more subject that consensus is to change and the less noticeable will be the effects of such changes on the life of the culture as a whole.

The deep structure and the surface structure within any culture form a continuum; the deep structure explains or accounts for the surface structure. Conceptually, it is altogether possible to demarcate different levels or zones on that continuum—some consensuses are more deeply embedded in a culture's way of life than others—but the more important point is that in every vital and cohesive culture there will be found to be a systematic congruence between deep and surface consensuses. Thus, for example, in a culture in which there is a deep-structure consensus on the value of efficiency and organization, there will most likely be a surface-structure consensus on the need to start and conclude even leisure-time events and friendly social calls on time. Furthermore, although it is the understanding of the deep-structure consensuses that will ultimately be more revealing, illuminating, and powerful for culture learning, it is often the case that the deep structure can be known only through the evidence manifested in the surface structure. The only way, for example, to know whether a genuine deep structure consensus exists within a culture on the importance of human rights and individual liberties is to observe and determine how these rights and liberties are protected and advanced in the surface structure by the laws, the courts, and other social institutions.

Having considered in this chapter the nature of culture learning and some of the distinctions necessary to understand this concept, we turn now to the first of the major modes of humanistic culture learning. Each of these modes of culture learning is considered major or basic precisely because it plays such an important role in the understanding of a culture's deep structure.

NOTES

1. Ralph Linton, *The Cultural Background of Personality* (New York: Appleton-Century-Crofts, 1945), p. 19.

2. Ibid., p. 19.

3. Nathan Glazer, "Liberty, Equality, Fraternity, Ethnicity," *Daedalus* 105 (Fall, 1976): 120.

4. Arnold J. Toynbee, *A Study of History,* vol. 12: *Reconsiderations* (London: Oxford University Press, 1961), p. 632.

5. Marx wrote: "This socialism is the declaration of the permanence of the revolution, the class dictatorship of the proletariat as the necessary transit point to the abolition of class distinctions generally, to the abolition of all the social relations that correspond to these relations of production, to the revolutionizing of all the ideas that result from these social relations." *On Revolution,* ed. and trans. Saul K. Radner (New York: McGraw-Hill, 1971), p. 226.

6. Ibid., p. 65.

7. Maurice Merleau-Ponty, *The Primacy of Perception and Other Essays,* ed. James M. Edie (Evanston, Ill.: Northwestern University Press, 1964).

8. As Plato argues in his famous allegory of the cave in Book VII of *The Republic,* all perceptions depend in large measure on the situation of the ones perceiving. The prisoners in Plato's cavelike underground dwelling could see only the shadows of artificial things cast by the fires. According to Plato, learning of any kind is not putting knowledge which is not in the mind into the mind, like putting sight into blind eyes. Rather, learning—and this would include culture learning—is the turning from "that which is *coming into being* together with the whole soul until it is able to endure looking at that which *is.*" *The Republic of Plato,* trans. Allan Bloom (New York: Basic Books, 1968), p.

197. More modern learning theory would speak of learning *"gestalts."* Culture learning is further complicated by the fact that *that which is,* namely, that which is to be learned or the cultural consensuses, does not necessarily correspond with anything *real* or *archetypal* in the Platonic sense.

9. Sigmund Freud, *Civilization and Its Discontents,* ed. and trans. James Strachey (New York: W. W. Norton & Company, 1961), p. 91.

10. John C. Condon, "Introduction," in *Intercultural Encounters with Japan,* ed. John C. Condon and Mitsuko Saito (Tokyo: The Simul Press, 1974), p. 4.

# chapter 3

# Cultural Continuity

In the first two chapters, we considered the nature of culture and culture learning, stressing how important these concepts are as a way of developing on one hand open-mindedness toward world-wide human perspectives and on the other an awareness of one's own cultural heritage and identity. Both broader outward views and deeper inward views are required by today's and tomorrow's interdependent world. In the chapters that follow we will study some of the major modes of culture learning, emphasizing not what culture learning is but how one might go about learning a culture. The modes of culture learning to be examined are those crucial to an understanding of a culture's deep structure. It might be remembered that a culture's deep structure gives rise to its surface structure, that is, accounts for, explains, and supports the more readily apparent and observable consensuses.

The first of these modes of culture learning is the historical mode. It is assumed in what follows that the culture learner has already decided which culture he or she wants to learn. It might be Chinese culture, American culture, Hawaiian culture, Pakistani culture, or whatever. It could also be a purely historical culture, that is, one now extinct except for its vestiges as they exist in material artifacts and in those broader influences it might have had on the development of subsequent cultures. The study even of cultures that no longer exist, such as Sumerian culture, can serve well to create in students those qualities of mind and heart that will equip them for participating fully in tomorrow's world. In the study of historical cultures, as was pointed out earlier, there is no possibility of an experiential component; there is no way that a student can live among the Sumerians of the tenth century B.C. Yet it would be a big mistake to think that learning such cultures is of interest only to antiquarians.

One thing that should be made clear at the beginning is that we are not discussing in this chapter the history of culture learning. Fascinating though that subject might be, including as it does the accounts of the great explorers, adventurers, conquerors, and "sojourners" as well as the more scientific works of anthropologists and ethnographers, it is not our concern at the moment. The history of culture learning as a whole has yet to be written. What we are investigating are ways in which knowing the history of a culture, its past, can help us to understand the consensuses on opinion and behavior that constitute that culture's way of life in the present. Whether or not one begins the learning of a culture by studying its past, one inevitably ends up feeling the need to explore how the culture came to be what it is today. Every existing culture is what it is now by reason of what it has accepted or rejected from its past; therefore one's learning of a culture is likely to be distorted, and it is sure to be incomplete, if the culture's history is ignored. The nature of a culture's deep structure requires that it be closely related to those thought and behavior patterns regarded as having been successful in the past and appropriate for the present. Keeping in mind the fact that the objective of the culture learner is not the same objective as that of the professional historian, three aspects of a culture's history are of special interest and value in culture learning: (1) the culture's historical accounts, (2) the culture's sense of history, and (3) how the people of the culture look upon or interpret their past.

## The Culture's Historical Accounts

Arnold Toynbee clarifies a point about the writing of history that many laypeople find difficult to comprehend. It is a point also ignored by some historians. Toynbee is trying to refute the idea that an historical account, even one given by an eyewitness to the event, is a description of what *really* or *objectively* happened. He writes: "Any historian will inevitably be living and working in a particular social milieu at a particular stage of its development, and his own situation will make him sensitive to some features in a past situation and blind to others."[1] If even scientifically trained historians are selectively sensitive to information, how much truer must this be of those historians who have not had the advantage of scientific training. Yet every culture has within it persons who are regarded, officially or unofficially, as custodians of the past, as those who come to feel responsible for keeping the legends and historical explanations alive so that they can be passed on to the next generation.

Unlike the historian, however, the culture learner is not particularly interested in whether these custodians of the past are reliable and more or less objective. If it is a culture with an oral tradition, the culture learner wants to know how that tradition has been carried on and to what extent its content still influences thought and behavior in the culture. If the culture has a written tradition, the culture learner wants to know which writings are still respected, revered, and widely read. He seeks more to discover what events have come to be accepted by the people themselves as historically important turning points rather than whether these were, in some objective sense, accurate descriptions. Unlike many historians, the culture learner is as much interested in finding out what the major consensuses were on opinion and behavior during normal, stable, or ordinary historical times as he is in finding out how the people reacted to great wars, dynastic overthrows, and natural disasters. The culture learner is particularly interested in discovering the great teachers and heroes of the culture's past; that the culture still honors what they said and did tells us much about what is deeply rooted in the culture's way of thinking and doing.

That cultures have different longevities is, of course, well established. The origin of the human race itself and of its earliest culture or cultures is still a matter for speculation. We have no clear knowledge of the very earliest cultures, but it is only logical—indeed somewhat tautological—to assume that the earliest cultures were not much preoccupied with the past. Some cultures must have begun virtually *de novo*. Some still-existing cultures, the Japanese for example, trace their heritage back thousands of years, while others, such as the American culture, are still relatively new. Some cultures have shown remarkable sustaining and revitalizing power, while others have changed so drastically that the older culture can be said to have vanished. The Greek and Roman cultures of classical times, for example, have left profound imprints on subsequent cultures, but they no longer exert the leadership they once did; thus classical Greek and Latin are known as dead languages and the glories of Greece and Rome are referred to in the past tense.

However long or short the people of a culture regard their history to be, the culture contains an account or accounts of a beginning, a time when the group first identified itself as a "we." The "we" or the in-group would be all of those people who think and behave in one way, and the "they" or the out-group would be those who think and behave in other ways. Before written or recorded history, the accounts of these beginnings would be transmitted by word of mouth from generation to generation, often in the form of stories, legends, and myths. According to the dictionary, both the words "tale" and "story" are archaic meanings of the word "history." These accounts would range all the way from how "we" were given the gift of fire to how "our" first ruler showed superhuman power; from how "we" perfected wet rice farming to how "our" victory in such and such a battle assured our independence. It appears essential to the viability of a culture that it have a recognized tradition, stemming from those beginnings, which the present generation accepts as its own and values sufficiently to preserve for posterity. One of the main purposes of this tradition or heritage is to unite the people of the culture in the feeling that they have a shared or common past—whether it be a past of positive glory and great achievements or a past filled with heroic suffering, at the hands of human enemies or of material forces, that needs at some future date to be avenged and righted. Cultures seem especially to need some account of a "Golden Age"[2] which their formal or informal historians hold in memory and keep alive, perhaps in hopes that such an age will come again, but also to serve as a moral standard against which to measure the culture's present health and spirit.

Further, the people of a culture are likely to be suspicious of any history of their origins and development related or written by someone outside that culture, even if they have no specific reason to doubt that person's motives or integrity. The thought that someone from outside the culture cannot fully understand, interpret, or do justice to a culture's history is probably based on the realization that an outsider may not consider important the same things the culture itself does.

We have already mentioned that history writing is always a matter of selection and emphasis and that even no insider can know a culture's history as it *really* was. But history is also a matter of meaning and significance, an art rather than a science, and the inside historian will be credited with seeing "our" history as we want or would like it to be seen. Thus, to take just one clear and perhaps oversimplified example, Americans are likely to feel that a history of America written by a Japanese scholar is necessarily lacking in "innerness" or perspective from within, although the Japanese public may regard it as an excellent interpretation of America. And conversely, the Japanese are likely to feel that a history of Japan written by an American scholar is lacking specifically the "Japaneseness" that would make it a good history, although the American public may regard it as an accurate and penetrating historical account of Japan.

A culture's account of itself—of how it came to be, what it has achieved, and what it has endured—ordinarily is in large part an account of the persons who have most profoundly influenced and shaped the consensuses on opinion and behavior that constitute that culture. These are the culture heroes, the persons whose opinions and behaviors become the models for other persons in the culture to emulate; these are the founders and the fathers of the culture as it used to be and as it has become. These are the persons most frequently quoted, after whom cities, parks, schools, streets, and roadways are named, and in whose memories statues are erected. These are the people most admired and respected in ordinary times and the people to whom the culture turns for leadership in times of crisis. The people of all cultures appear to find it much easier to identify with human models than with abstract ideas.

Freud's important point that a culture's heroes are not at all its most well-balanced and representative members will serve as a caution to culture learners. Heroes and geniuses are such precisely because they stand out from the majority and give direction to the majority's thinking and behaving. Freud wrote: "The super-ego of an epoch of civilization has an origin similar to that of an individual. It is based on the impression left behind by the personalities of great leaders—men of overwhelming force of mind or men in whom one of the human impulsions has found its strongest and purest, and therefore often its most one-sided, expression."[3]

One of the culture learner's main tasks is to seek to discover what correspondence there is between the culture's historical accounts of itself and of its heroes and leaders and the opinions and behaviors of the people generally in the culture. To what extent, for example, did George Washington and Thomas Jefferson really speak for the people of revolutionary America and to what extent do they still speak to and for Americans today? The culture's historical account of itself, centering around its leaders and heroes, will be of little value to the culture learner if these persons have lived on only in history books and have not deeply touched the thinking and the behaviors of the people. To take another example: Mao Tse-tung has certainly exercised great influence over contemporary China, but does this influence really mean that Confucianism has disappeared or will disappear? Does the fact that a culture or a country considers itself Christian or Buddhist or Islamic, to take another example, really mean that religious thinking shapes the consensuses on opinion and behavior, or might it not be possible that the culture is Christian, Buddhist, or Islamic in name only? Put somewhat too bluntly, the culture learner seeks to discover what thinking and values of the past are truly at work in the culture as contrasted with those that are simply reported to be. The culture learner can safely assume there is some measure of congruity between opinion and behavior in every culture. Neither individuals nor whole cultures behave randomly in the present as if there were no past and no purpose in the future. But there is no certain way in which the culture learner can know what thoughts from the past are still influencing a culture's thought and behavior in the present. Without in any way intending to deceive, the people of a culture can easily conceal their real thinking, and they may behave in certain ways simply because they think they are expected to behave that way. For one example, a culture learner might erroneously conclude that voting or nonvoting patterns in a particular culture were closely related to historical thinking about the value of democracy when in fact voting or not voting might be directly related only to the question of whether fines are imposed on those who do not vote. Or, for another example, a culture learner might be led by reading statistics or by observing how many people go to church regularly in a given culture to conclude that religious observance is or is not deeply rooted in the life of the people. But on one hand, going to church might be primarily for social or recreational purposes; on the other, deeply religious people might stay away from church for fear of offending certain ruling political regimes.

Although the insights to be derived from historical study of a culture are of immense value for culture learning, and although interviewing and public opinion polling techniques have been greatly improved, the culture learner faces a major difficulty in attempting to learn a culture's past. The natural and understandable inclination of the official and unofficial custodians of the past within any culture to try to tell the people what they want the people to hear—or what the people want to hear—is well known. This inclination takes two forms: (1) the mythologizing of those people and events of the past that are currently in favor, and (2) the demythologizing of those people and events that are not currently in favor. To take just one example of each: Parson Weems was so anxious to make George Washington an idol for all Americans, including the school children, that he made up a number of stories extolling Washington's physical and spiritual virtues.[4] Some of these are still current in American juvenile histories on the grounds that even if Washington did not, for example, refuse to lie to his father about the cherry tree, there is no harm in anyone's thinking that he did. An opposite example: In the de-Stalinization period in Russian history, the name of Stalin was completely eliminated from the history textbooks used in the Russian schools.

### The Culture's Sense of History

In attempting to clarify the idea of culture learning through history, we have in previous sections considered briefly the culture's consensuses on what might be called "the facts" of its history or, in other words, the culture's own historical account of itself, of the main people and the main events in its recording of the past. We turn now to a closely related question that must also occupy the mind of the culture learner. This is the culture's present consensuses on its obligation to its past, its heritage, and its tradition. The culture's consensus on this matter, on its sense of the meaning and value of its history, will determine to a very large degree whether the culture is receptive to new ideas or whether it is mainly concerned with conserving the opinions and behaviors to which it has become accustomed and with which it feels satisfied. Major and drastic changes, at least in behavior, may always be forced on the people of any culture by well-organized minorities backed up by military and police power. Basic changes in a culture's way of seeing and doing things will also be brought about, with greater or lesser inevitability, by scientific and technological advances. But how much freely chosen change there will be is a function of the culture's self-image, as derived largely from its past.

A culture's "sense of history" means simply its consensus on how important, how highly to be treasured or valued, is its past. How heavily or lightly does the feeling for past ways of thinking and doing things rest on the shoulders of those now living? How much does the decision making that has to be done today rely on the wisdom of the ancients and on the premise that since this is the way it has been done "since the memory of man runneth not to the contrary," this is also the way it should be done today?

The consensus within a culture regarding how much importance is to be attached to established and consecrated ways of seeing and doing things does not appear to be determined only by how long the culture has been in existence. Some of the newer cultures are very conservative, even though they may have come into existence through revolutionary action. Nor does cultural conservation seem to be specifically related to whether or not the culture practices some form of ancestor worship, although ancestor worship has been a fairly common phenomenon and is based on the premise that ancestors remain in touch with subsequent live generations and influence their fortunes for good or ill. The culture will, however, tend to be more open or closed to new ideas depending on how much respect and attention is given within the culture to the opinions and ways of its older members. A culture in which the most important decisions are reserved to older people, whose lives are largely behind them, is much more likely to feel the full weight of the past than one in which younger people make major decisions, that is, hold high and responsible positions. It may be almost impossible to determine which is the cause and which the effect, whether a culture respects its elders because it respects its past or whether its respect of the past is generated by its respect for its elders.

A culture's sense of history is expressed in a number of ways, in the value that it puts, for example, on traditional holidays and festivals and on the proper ways of observing such customs. Or on the importance attached by the people of a culture to lineage and how far back individuals can trace their family tree. Or on the attention given to the preserving of historical monuments, ancient temples and churches, and burial grounds. Cultures have, in fact, long been stereotyped as traditional or progressive depending on whether they have been more concerned with glorifying the past than with changing the course of the future; as backward looking or forward looking depending on whether they took their advice and guidance from the wisdom of the past or from the use of reason and intelligence in sizing up the needs of the present and the opportunities for the future.

There are, however, two principal ways in which a culture learner comes to understand and appreciate a particular culture's sense of history or of the past. The first is through a study of how history is taught in the culture's schools, colleges, and universities, and the second is through an analysis of the kinds of laws that govern the behavior of the people of the culture. We will have occasion in the chapter on *The Rule of Law* to examine the second of these in greater depth; here we need to consider only the broad outline of the concept. The first way, how history is taught and emphasized in the schools, colleges, and universities, requires some extensive consideration.

One of the main purposes of any culture's system of laws is to give permanence, cohesion, and stability to the culture. It is the legal system, whether extensive and highly articulated or minimal and barely distinguishable from the accepted mores and folkways, that allows the people of the culture to know what they can expect of other persons and what will be expected of them. The culture's sense of history will be revealed clearly both in who makes the laws and in who enforces them. Thus, for example, the people of a culture with a consitutional type of government will be found to have reached some kind of a consensus on whether the constitution itself is permanent, inviolable, and sacrosanct of whether it is flexible and easily modified as social and economic conditions change.[5] Thus too the people with a common law tradition will have a broad consensus on how rigidly a judge is to adhere to precedent—or *stare decisis*—and how much he is free to deviate from precedent and thus make new laws. The laws and the system of government they create are one of the clearest expressions of a culture's sense of history because, to the extent they are based on reasoning and experience, they draw on the past by their very nature. The laws simply cannot in practice be completely wiped away so that each new day or even each new generation can make its own laws. Even revolutionary governments have to draw to some extent on the traditions of the people and their feeling about what should and should not be included in the laws, if the revolution is to be anything more than a temporary one.

A culture's sense of history, however, reflects itself most directly and clearly in the emphasis placed on history in the curriculum of the formal educational insitutions and in the way or manner in which history is taught. The deep sense of history is also revealed in some cultures, not so much in the formal classroom as in the stories that are told, the dances performed, the artifacts that are preserved and treasured, the dramas presented, and the ancient classical poems that are repeated on holidays and festival days. The children learn of their past and the adults are reminded of their origins and background in ways that are both emotionally and intellectually appealing. The culture also reveals whether or not it has a strong sense of the importance of the past in the number of "evocations of the past" that are found in novels, folksongs, traditional ballads, morality plays, and biographies.

Nonetheless, it is through the history textbooks and other historical reference sources used in the schools, colleges, and universities that the culture learner most readily comes to an understanding of the culture's sense of the past. Those responsible for determining how much history should be taught and required, what kinds of history will be taught, and in what ways represent not only the present culture's sense of its own past history and that of other culture, but also what sense of history the future generations will have. Thus, if there is a consensus in the culture that history is important—if not in itself, at least as a guide to making sure that the mistakes of the past are not repeated—then history will be stressed in the schools. It will have a prominent place in both the required and the elective curriculum. On the other hand, if the culture has no consensus on the relative importance of history, that subject matter will find its way into the general curriculum only in a minor way. The process of building any school curriculum is basically one of selecting out from the great volume and variety of "all knowledge" that knowledge regarded as most valuable and essential.

A strong consensus within a culture on the importance of history will manifest itself in the teaching and learning of what might be called *political history*, but it will also go far beyond this, making history a dimension of all studies and of life itself. In some cultures, history is thought to be largely the study of wars, conquests, and invasions—in short, the study of the struggle for power among or between governments. History, then, becomes a kind of specialized study, a subject in itself, rather than a mode or a perspective necessary in the consideration of any or all problems. It is entirely possible, consequently, for us to find cultures in which the study of "political history" may be both highly developed and required of all or most students, and yet we would have to conclude that the people of that culture do not have a strong consensus on the importance of history. The people as a whole may well have come to conclude that the histories of those persons who have rank and power have very little importance for daily living. The culture learner also gets a strong clue about the culture's consensus on the importance of history simply by noting how history is divided—for example, ancient, medieval, and modern—and determining when the modern period is thought to have begun. If the ancients are studied as intensively as the moderns and if the concept of historical studies embraces all of the culture's people and all of its problems—not just its wars—then the culture learner safely concludes that the culture has a strong sense of history.

It is to be expected that different cultures will give first priority, among all possible historical studies, to the history of the culture or society of which the teacher and the students are themselves members. Even if history is not generally stressed in the curriculum, some place will ordinarily be found for a certain amount of study of one's own culture. School authorities in every culture will insist that every student have the opportunity, indeed the obligation, to study the people and the events that made the culture what it is today. In some cultures, the sense of history is simply the same as "a sense of our own history." In the past, educators have complained frequently and often bitterly about how uninformed and misinformed the people of the West were about the history and the achievements of Eastern peoples, and vice versa. This is, of course, largely still true, but an important new movement is underway now in the area of history writing and history teaching-learning that may lead eventually to the resolution of this difficulty. The movement is toward the writing of "world history." This movement is particularly significant because it places individual culture learning in its broadest context without in any way minimizing the need to study individual cultures in their depths.

## How Cultures Interpret Their Past

The culture learner is especially concerned with how the people of a given culture see and interpret their past. Do they see themselves as having conducted themselves well or poorly in their relationships with the people of other cultures? Do they see themselves as having been generally exploited or victimized in the course of history, or do they see themselves as having been more or less masters of their own fate? Do they see themselves as having made important contributions to the advancement of human civilization? Do they see themselves as more preoccupied with great moral and spiritual questions or with material needs, goods, and possessions? Just as an individual has a certain view of his own family background, which might range all the way from great pride to varying degrees of rejection, so too do the people of a culture as a whole. The individual's view of his background is, of course, largely determined by what he or she perceives, hears, and senses by living in the culture itself. The consensus within a culture regarding how the past should be interpreted will find expression, among other things, in the rituals carried on within the culture. Michael Polanyi, author of *Personal Knowledge Towards a Post-Critical Philosophy,* puts the idea this way: "By fully participating in a ritual, the members of a group affirm the community of their existence, and at the same time identify the life of their group with antecedent groups, from whom the ritual has descended to them. Every ritual act of a group is to this extent a reconciliation within the group and a reestablishment of continuity with its own history as a group."[6]

This point about learning the consensus within a culture regarding how the culture views its past is perhaps better illustrated than described. We therefore turn now for purposes of illustration to three contemporary cultures in which a particular view of the past is expressed itself with great clarity. These are: (1) Judaic culture, with a covenant view of the past, (2) American culture, with an eclectic and pragmatic view of the past, (3) Chinese culture, with a cyclic and ceremonial view of the past. Other cultures will, of course, view their own past in different ways. The point stressed here is nothing more than that some "view of the past" is one of the formative elements in the deep structure of all cultures.

## Judaic Culture

The Judaic people have interpreted their past as one in which Yahweh or Jehovah entered into a special covenant with them and only with them. In this sense, they were chosen or selected by Yahweh or Jehovah as his special people and for his special purposes. The Hebrew people and their leaders had implicit faith that Jehovah would sustain them through their vicissitudes if only they were obedient to their side of the covenant. Jehovah, on his side, being almighty and all powerful, could not fail to live up to his side of the covenant. This covenant itself was an unchanging eternal presence that required its own location and treatment in the ark of the covenant.

The point of greatest interest here is that the Judaic people saw the historical act of entering into a covenant with Jehovah as conferring a unique status on them as a group. The people of other cultures, not having been party to the covenant, were not chosen or selected by Jehovah—at least not in the same way. Their covenant gave the Jewish people not only a purpose and destiny other peoples could not share but also an extraordinarily facile way of accounting for whatever good or bad fortune that would befall them in their long history. All good things that came to them did so because of Jehovah's recognition of their fidelity to the covenant; misfortune or evil came because of Jehovah's displeasure with the way they were thinking or behaving. At the same time that the covenant strongly united the Hebrew people among themselves, it set them apart from other people. Theirs was a special dispensation and a unique role that carried with it a special way of thinking and behaving.

Another interesting aspect of the Judaic interpretation of their cultural past is that the special dispensation they regarded themselves as enjoying went with them wherever they might go. The covenant between Jehovah and the Judaic people was not a territorial but a personal one; it did not bind both Jehovah and the Judaic people only so long as the Jewish people remained in Palestine, their country or homeland in Biblical times. The Judaic people were in fact driven from their homeland and they scattered throughout much of the world. Judaic culture, as well as the dream of someday returning to their own homeland, went with them. (Judaic culture, incidentally, might be categorized as both a horizontal and a vertical culture, as these terms were explained in chapter 1.)

Whether there is a consensus within Judaic culture that a return to the homeland is an essential part of the culture itself is probably debatable. But as Palmer D. Edmunds states, "From the sixteenth century on there was a noticeable return of Jews to Palestine. A trickle at first, persecution in Russia and other places initiated a flow of refugees which grew at a modest rate. The nineteenth century witnessed the formation of the World

Zionist Organization, which promoted a program of Palestinian resettlement."[7]

The question of the "homeland" and how a culture views its past is interestingly posed by the people of the Judaic culture but is actually part of a much more general problem. The people of some cultures see their past as inseparable from preserving the "homeland," on the theory that cultural continuity means existence throughout time in a particular place. The people of other cultures see their past as one in which a break with the "homeland" was the decisive event. These people, whatever their reasons for leaving their original homeland, usually come in the course of time to consider the land in which they live their homeland. A culture's view of its past, therefore, may be thought of as involving both a time or generational dimension and a place or homeland dimension.

## American Culture

Having now celebrated the Bicentennial of the signing of the Declaration of Independence, America can no longer be considered a new country. True, Hawaii, the fiftieth state, was added to the Union as late as 1959, but compared with a number of new nations created since World War II, America has already had a considerable history and experience as a nation. American culture on the whole, however, is selected here as an example of a culture which is much more forward looking than backward looking. The past is recalled through periodic ceremonial observances—the Bicentennial, for example—but even as such ceremonies are taking place, the American people are busy planning and preparing for the future. In the pragmatic American view, what is past is past; it is not dishonored, but neither is it allowed to frustrate newer ways of thinking and doing things. Progress is seen as a result of willingness to break with the past and try the new.

Apart from that small but influential group of New England colonists who had a prophetlike vision of establishing the Kingdom of God in the New World, the early Americans did not see their past as one in which they had been in any way chosen. Many of those who came to America did so to escape a past filled with oppression, exploitation, tyranny, and persecution. They saw themselves as fortunate, perhaps blessed, responsible for making the most of their opportunities, but not weighed down by ancient forms or traditions. Their constitutional fathers had a sense of mission; free of the feudalistic oppressions of the Old World, they longed to see whether the new concept of democracy, as they conceived it, might work. Richard B. Morris, president of the American Historical Association during the Bicentennial year, states: "Our restraint should spring not from fear but rather from a deep-felt recognition that our experiment in government, which the Bicentennial commemorates, is still the last best hope of mankind."[8] Traced only a relatively few generations back, the American past is in fact made up of many "pasts." American culture finds its unity, in part, in the hope it holds out to all for a brighter future.

There is at least one major ambiguity in the way the people of the American culture view their past. By and large, Americans are experiential, eager to improve and, often enough, willing to change just for the sake for change. As has been indicated, there is little obeisance to the past in the sense of feeling bound by it or even very strongly related to it. Yet Americans have an almost sacred regard for the Constitution of the United States. Realizing fully that the Constitution is a manmade document and that it can be—and has been—amended, Americans are firmly committed to the inviolability of a Constitution which will soon be 200 years old. The final acid test of any proposed legislation, for example, is whether it conforms with the spirit and substance of the Constitution.

It is probably safe to say that there is a consensus in American culture on the fact that Americans can look to the past with some measure of justifiable pride. The system of self-government, with all its shortcomings, seems still to work reasonably well. This pride derives not so much from the country's size and strength but from its social and political philosophy, the basic ideas and values of which took root in the past and, as appropriately modified, have been handed down from generation to generation. There is, for example, no significant number of Americans seeking to leave the country permanently to find a better life elsewhere.

It became clear, however, especially in all that was said and written at the time of the American Bicentennial celebrations, that Americans view their past with mixed emotions. Running concurrently and almost as deeply and broadly as the consensus on a justifiable national pride is a consensus on the fact that the historical record shows a huge gap between American ideals and American realities. Having been taught a primary lesson by their forefathers that the forces of history are not inexorable, that is, that intelligence and strong determination can make a difference in human affairs, Americans tend to be less tolerant and understanding than they might otherwise be when they examine certain parts of the legacy and tradition handed down to them. They are as critical of historical blunders and mistakes as they are pleased with historical achievements.

Americans, in short, spend much more time considering what can and should be done to meet the challenges of the present and the future than they do worrying about what could or should have been done in the past. They see the circumstances of history as only one of the factors—and not the most important—involved in solving the problems faced by this generation, and they expect future generations to feel the same way.

### Pre-1949 Chinese Culture

The third illustration is that of China prior to the Communist revolutionary takeover in 1949. Chinese culture was so deeply rooted in history that the past could be said to dominate and determine all of its major aspects. It is interesting to observe that even contemporary Chinese Communist theorists have trouble deciding, for example, whether to purge Confucius or claim him as one of the earliest forerunners of the Chinese version of Marxist-Leninist thought. The people of the earlier Chinese culture had looked reverently on its past, not because of any thought that they had been especially chosen or selected, but simply because they thought it was the source of greatest wisdom and they had much to learn from it. *Chung-kuo,* the English word for which is "China," means "Central Nation." The Chinese regarded themselves as inhabiting a land which was at the center or the hub of the universe, and they viewed others who were not a part of the central nation as outsiders, if not barbarians. The Chinese culture, unlike the American culture, was not the result of exploration, settlement, and the coming together of people from many different lands to form an overarching common culture. China became a unified culture very early, and it may well be that China has had such a strong feeling for the past ever since principally simply because the Chinese people were in fact able to achieve high standards of civilization.

During the Shang dynasty, which is traditionally dated as beginning in 1766 B.C., the Chinese developed bronze metallurgy, made glazed pottery of the finest quality, and carved jade into highly artistic shapes and forms. At this time as well, the Chinese arrived at a nonphonetic language which is the oldest surviving language in use in the world. Agriculture was also already highly developed. Subsequent generations of Chinese had good reason to look back with admiration on the ways of thinking and behaving that had gone before.

Passing reference has already been made to Confucius. Joseph Needham, the eminent scholar of Chinese culture, writes of him: " . . . there may have been some before Confucius who taught doctrines similar to his, but none who by force of character and originality of mind, succeeded as he did in impressing their conceptions and personality upon all following generations."[9] The point of greatest importance, moreover, in understanding the Chinese view of the past is that even Confucius himself looked upon the past with utmost respect. According to Needham, Confucius, who called himself a transmitter and not an originator, called for a return to the "way of the Sage Kings." Confucius clothed his ethical insights with legendary historical authority.

Dun J. Li, in his book *The Ageless Chinese,* explains that Confucian philosophy may account for the unique historical-mindedness of the Chinese. The Chinese or Confucian view of the past may be called a cyclic or ceremonial view of the past precisely because it does not recognize any hard and fast or distinct differences between the past and the present. Li writes:

> According to Confucian philosophers, there were five cardinal rela-
> tionships among men. . . . All of these relationships were between

superiors and inferiors, and even among friends the older was supposedly superior to the younger. The relationships did not cease with the death of the party involved; theoretically at least, they lasted indefinitely. The ancestors of a reigning emperor were revered by the nation as a whole, and the greatest men of the past were worshipped throughout history. . . . Ancestors were worshipped long after their death; the older the generation to which they belonged, the more they honored.[10]

Needham points out that Confucius taught a doctrine of "this-worldly social-mindedness." Man was literally the measure of all things. What shaped or determined the culture, then, in its very essence was " . . . that body of customs which the sage-kings and the people has always accepted, i.e., what the Confucians called *li*."[11] The Chinese accepted the past and regarded it as both formative and important because only there could they find the body of customs passed down by the sage-kings and the people. This penchant for looking to the past for wisdom and direction found expression at the practical level in the widespread use of proverbs among the Chinese. And as John King Fairbanks, famed historian of China, writes: "Human society and personal relationships continued to be the focus of Chinese learning, not the conquest of man over nature."[12]

Every existing culture is necessarily the result or the product of the ideas and the ways of doing things that went into its formation and development. Cultures change more or less rapidly, but the speed and direction of change depend in part on the past. In this chapter we have sought to discover how the culture learner gains insights into the deep structure of the culture by studying the culture's historical account of itself, by analyzing the culture's sense of history, and by determining how the culture interprets or evaluates its past, that is, the image it holds of itself. We have seen, in the examples of Judaic culture, American culture, and Chinese culture, that these self-images vary greatly from culture to culture. We have stressed the point that one cannot know a culture without knowing what that culture was in the past; its present identity is largely determined by what its past has been, and its future will be largely determined by what it perceives itself to be in the present.

NOTES

1. Arnold Toynbee, *A Study of History,* vol. 12: *Reconsiderations* (London: Oxford University Press,1961), p. 51.

2. Mircea Eliade explores this phenomenon in detail in chapter 6, "Paradise and Utopia," of his *The Quest* (Chicago: University of Chicago Press, 1969), pp. 88–111. He uses the pioneer American culture and the Tupi-Guarani's tribal culture of Brazil as examples and case studies.

3. Sigmund Freud, *Civilization and Its Discontents,* ed. and trans. James Strachey (New York: W. W. Norton & Company, 1961), p. 88.

4. "Needless to say, historical students may not accept one man's conclusion that this story is true and that false. The standard is as frail as judgment is feeble." Douglas Southall Freeman, *George Washington: A Biography,* vol. 1 (New York: Charles Scribner's Sons, 1948), xx.

5. John Rawls in his excellent *A Theory of Justice* (Cambridge, Mass.: The Belknap Press of Harvard University Press,1971) relates the form of law in a society far back in its past to an original social contract. He writes: "My aim is to present a conception of justice which generalizes and carries to a high level of abstraction the familiar theory of the social contract as found, say, in Locke, Rousseau, Kant. . . . they are the principles that free and rational persons concerned to further their own interests would accept in an initial position of equality as defining the fundamental terms of their association. These principles are to regulate all further agreements; they specify the kinds of social cooperation that can be entered into and the forms of government that can be established" (p. 11).

6. Michael Polanyi, *Personal Knowledge Towards a Post-Critical Philosophy* (Chicago: University of Chicago Press,1962), p. 211.

7. Palmer D. Edmunds, *Law and Civilization* (Washington, D.C.: Public Affairs Press, 1969), p. 212.

8. Richard B. Morris, "The American Revolution and Asia," unpublished paper presented at the East-West Center Bicentennial Seminar, "The American Revolution: Its Meaning to Asians and Americans," June 28, 1976, p. 34.

9. Joseph Needham, *Science and Civilisation in China,* vol. 2: *History of Scientific Thought* (Cambridge: Cambridge University Press, 1956), p. 5.

10. Dun J. Li, *The Ageless Chinese,* 2nd ed. (New York: Charles Scribner's Sons, 1971), p. 69.

11. Needham, *Science and Civilisation,* p. 521.

12. John King Fairbanks, *The United States and China,* 3rd ed. (Cambridge, Mass.: Harvard University Press,1971), p. 68.

*chapter* 4
# Culture Learning and Language Learning

We are concerned here with what a culture is and humanistic ways to learn it. We have noted earlier that a culture may be seen as a specific, though extremely complex, *subject matter to be learned* in much the same way as physics, music, or international relations are subject matters to be learned. What precisely is to be learned are the consensuses on opinion and behavior that constitute, define, and identify a culture. Because cultures are consensuses, they are intelligible and comprehensible, something that can be learned. We know as a fact of experience that people learn their own cultures, and we can point to numberless examples of persons who have learned one or more cultures in addition to their own.

The question arises immediately whether it is possible fully to learn another culture without learning the language used in that culture. (The learning of one's own culture inevitably entails the learning of the language.) Put broadly, the question is one of the relationships between culture learning and language learning. Put more specifically, the question is whether a person can learn a particular culture, Japanese culture for example, without learning to read and write Japanese.

For reasons that we will examine in this chapter, the answer to the question of whether it is possible fully to learn a culture without learning its language would be *no*. The emphatic word here is *fully,* but strictly speaking the word *fully* cannot be applied to the process of culture learning. In culture learning, as in all other kinds of learning, there is always something further to be learned. Culture learning, like learning of any kind, is a matter of degrees or of progress on a continuum rather than something that might be added up to reach an imaginary 100 percent. No person can ever learn a culture fully, no matter how proficient that person might be in its language. So the question must mean, "Can a person learn a culture *well* without knowing that culture's language?" The answer is a qualified *yes.*

One way of stating the relationship between language learning and culture learning is: All other things being equal, the person who knows the language of a culture will be able to learn that culture much more readily, directly, and fully than the person who does not know that language. Language learning is an immensely helpful and exceptionally powerful tool in culture learning, but it is not absolutely necessary to genuine culture learning![1]

We must also keep in mind that spoken and written language is only one form of communication and not necessarily the most effective means of communication at all. Human beings often communicate both their ideas and their feelings in many nonverbal ways. Paul Wetzlawich, Janet Helmick Beavin, and Don D. Jackson make an important distinction between *digital* communication (verbal), in which the intention is to make denotative statements about objects, and *analogic* communication (nonverbal), in which the intention is to define the relationship between those entering into the communication. They state:

> Indeed, wherever relationship is the central issue of communication, we find that digital communication is almost meaningless. This is not only the case between animals and between man and animal, but in many other contingencies in human life, e.g., courtship, love, succor, combat, and, of course, in all dealings with very young children or severely disturbed mental patients. Children, fools, and animals have always been credited with particular intuition regarding the sincerity or insincerity of human attitudes, for it is easy to profess something verbally, but difficult to carry a lie into the realm of the analogic.[2]

The authors give a good illustration of the difference between digital or verbal communication and analogic or nonverbal communication in pointing out that no amount of listening to a foreign language on the radio will yield an understanding of the language, whereas some basic information can fairly easily be derived from watching sign language and from so-called intention movements, including gesture, even when used by a person of a totally different culture.

## Language, a Part of Culture

The main reason that learning the language of a culture is so helpful to learning the culture itself is that language and culture are not separable in reality. There is not one thing to be called a culture and another to be called "the language of that culture," just as there is not one thing to be called "a culture" and another thing to be called "the history of the culture." Just as a culture, a way of life or a set of consensuses on opinion and behavior, is what it is because of its history, so it is what it is because of its language. If a culture had a different history or a different language, it would be an altogether different culture from what it is.

Benjamin Lee Whorf, as a result of his intensive study of the morphology of the Hopi Indian language, is often credited with having given the most credibility to the hypothesis that the language system of a culture determines to a very large extent the general thought and behavior patterns of that culture. In fact, however, Clyde and Florence Kluckhohn, working among the Navahos, had earlier recorded the same insight. Whorf himself quotes the conclusions of Edward Sapir, under whom he studied, on this very point:

> Human beings do not live in the objective world alone, nor alone in the world of social activity as ordinarily understood, but are very much at the mercy of the particular language which has become the medium of expression for their society. It is quite an illusion to imagine that one adjusts to reality essentially without the uses of language and that language is merely an incidental means of solving specific problems of communication or reflection. The fact of the matter is that the "real world" is to a large extent unconsciously built up on the language habits of the group. . . . We see and hear and otherwise experience very largely as we do because the language

habits of our community predispose certain choices of interpretation.[3]

This hypothesis, generally referred to as the "Whorfian Hypothesis," is not without its severe critics. Michael Cole and Sylvia
Scribner state: "It is probable that the majority of scholars would
agree in rejecting those of Whorf's formulations that stress the
*arbitrary* character of the language-experience relationship and
the inescapable and rigid constraints imposed on cognitive processes by language."[4] They conclude, however, that "in this
young and potentially rich field of investigation of how individuals use their language not only for social communication but as a
tool for thought, Whorf still lives."[5]

For almost two years Whorf studied the differences between
Western European languages (what he called SAE, or "Standard
Average European") and the Hopi language. This is not the
place to report his findings in detail, but he was able to show that
there are significant differences in the ways in which the SAE
and the Hopi view singulars and plurals, nouns of physical quan-
tity, phrases of cycles, temporal forms of verbs, and expressions
of duration, intensity, and tendency. This means that there are
also significant differences in the ways SAE and Hopi analyze,
classify, categorize, and report experience.

To take just one of Whorf's specific examples: After making
clear that the Hopi verbs for preparing do not correspond neatly
to SAE "prepare" and that the Hopi word *na' twani* could also
be rendered "the practiced-upon, the tried for," Whorf states
that the Hopi microcosm seems to have analyzed reality in terms
of events, or better, "eventing." He says that, for the Hopi,
everything that manifests itself as a definite whole has the power
to determine its own mode of duration: growth, decline, stability, cyclicity, or creativeness. "Everything is thus already 'prepared' for the way it now manifests by earlier phases, and what it
will be later, partly has been, and partly is in the act of being so
'prepared.' An emphasis and importance rests on this preparing
or being prepared aspect of the world that may to the Hopi correspond to that 'quality of reality' that matter or 'stuff' has for
us."[6]

Whorf shows that as a result of the Hopis' linguistic conditioning, an important characteristic of their behavior is the emphasis on preparation. He states that "this Hopi preparing behavior may be roughly divided into announcing, outer preparing, inner preparing, covert participation, and persistence."[7] Whorf's understanding of Hopi culture is beautifully summarized in his comment on the last of these preparing behaviors, namely, persistence. He says:

> Hopi "preparing" activities again show a result of their linguistic thought background in an emphasis on persistence and constant insistent repetition . . . to us for whom time is a motion on a space, unvarying repetition seems to scatter its force along a row of units of that space, and be wasted; to the Hopi, for whom time is not a motion but a "getting later" of everything that has ever been done, unvarying repetition is not wasted but accumulated. It is storing up an invisible change that holds over into later events. As we have seen, it is as if the return of the day were felt as the return of the same person, a little older but with all the impresses of yesterday, not as "another day," i.e. like an entirely different person.[8]

Whorf asks the general question: How does such a network of language, culture, and behavior come about historically? And: Which was first, the language patterns or the cultural norms? His answer is clear: "In main they have grown up together, constantly influencing each other. But in this partnership the nature of the language is the factor that limits free plasticity and rigidifies channels of development in the more autocratic way."[9]

## Deep Structure and Surface Structure

A second reason why learning a culture's language is basic to learning that culture is that a knowledge of the deep structure of the language leads to a knowledge of the deep structure of the culture. If for the moment we take the difference between the surface structure and the deep structure—in either a language or a culture—to be the difference between form and meaning, then it will be evident that the culture learner, like the language learner, is interested in much more than surface forms or the direct expressions or manifestations of the culture. The culture learner is, in fact, much more interested in the deeper meanings or explanations that underlie the surface appearances than he is in those appearances themselves. To take just two simple examples: In studying a culture that shows high regard and deference to its older people, the culture learner is much more concerned with determining why this should be the case than he is with simply recording his direct observations of the ways this characteristic manifests itself. Or in studying a culture in which religious observance or churchgoing plays an important part in the life of the people, the culture learner is much more interested in the explanation, interpretation, or meaning behind this phenomenon than he is in counting how many people go to church regularly or fast and pray at the appointed times.

While it is roughly true that the difference between surface structure and deep structure is the difference between form and meaning, further definition and description of the terms *surface structure* and *deep structure* is necessary. It must also be repeated for purposes of clarity that we are considering two different kinds of *surface structures* and *deep structures* here: (1) the surface structure and the deep structure of the culture itself, and (2) the surface structure and the deep structure of the culture's language. The point is that it is extremely difficult, if not impossible, to understand the deep structure of the culture unless one understands the deep structure of the culture's language. Or better—one of the most fruitful ways of coming to understand the deep structure of the culture is through an understanding of the deep structure of the language.

First, the concepts of surface structure and deep structure as they apply to the culture as a whole or in itself.

As Noam Chomsky has correctly pointed out: "We can be reasonably certain that investigation of direct relations between experience and action, between stimuli and responses, will in general be a vain pursuit. In all but the most elementary cases, what a person does depends in large measure on what he knows, believes, and anticipates. A study of human behavior that is not based on at least a tentative formulation of relevant systems of knowledge and belief is predestined to triviality and irrelevance."[10] The surface structure of a culture consists of those consensuses on opinion and behavior that are more or less observable by anyone who happens to look. The people of a given culture, for example, go to school or work on specific days, they wear certain kinds of clothes, they eat their meals at more or less fixed times and in more or less fixed ways, they find their leisure and recreation in culturally prescribed ways, and at night they sleep on the kinds of surfaces they have come to regard as comfortable. These are all part of the culture's patterns—they are various consensuses on opinion and behavior—but they are also only its surface structure, only that which appears and is manifest.

In contrast, the *deep structure* of a culture is, in Chomsky's words, the culture's relevant systems of knowledge and belief. The *deep structure* of the culture is that system of knowing, believing, and anticipating that explains, validates, legitimates, and integrates the culture as a whole. It is the deep structure that gives meaning to the forms that appear at the surface of the culture's way of life. The deep structure is what is behind, underneath, at the bottom of whatever of importance that happens in the culture. Because of the fundamental knowing, believing, and anticipating that takes place in the culture, some kinds of possible human behavior appear on the surface and other kinds do not.

A clear and relatively simple example will illustrate the concept of the deep structure of a culture. This illustration is intended to show both what the deep structure is and how knowledge, belief, and anticipations get into the culture's deep structure. Confucianism dominated Chinese culture for many hundreds of years and, as we have seen, still exerts great influence even in postrevolutionary China. The essence of the Confucian teaching was that *jen*, variably translated as benevolence, love, compassion, and the like, should be the principle that governs all the relationships among human beings. As Dun J. Li points out, *jen* "was derived from man's innate goodness, though outwardly it was manifested in a variety of forms."[11] Li goes on to explain that "goodness was implied in manhood; it needed no outside inducement. If a man performed good deeds for ulterior purposes, whether they be fame or wealth, his motives were not pure and there was little goodness in his deeds. *In fact, motives were more important than results* [italics added]."[12] The point to be noted, in considering the concept of a culture's *deep structure,* is not that the principle of *jen* was always faithfully practiced by the Chinese in their relationships with one another or with outsiders, but that the principle of *jen* became the norm against which all behavior was measured. If relationships among people were governed by *jen,* they were good (harmonious); if they were not governed by *jen,* they were bad (discordant, lacking in virtue or harmony).

The Confucian way of thinking, as taught first by Confucius himself and then by his much-respected interpreters, Mencius for example, came in the course of years to be more than one of the ways of thinking among the Chinese. It became precisely *the* Chinese way of thinking. It had entered the culture's *deep structure;* it came to be taken for granted in itself, and it served as the reference, norm, or basis of explanation for surface opinions and behaviors. Confucius was universally and frequently quoted by parents, teachers, and public officials. Confucianism informed the public conscience and consciousness to such an extent that his teachings were no longer publicly open to scrutiny and criticism, no matter how much scholars might dispute among themselves regarding what Confucius actually said and meant. Even the examinations used to determine who would and who would not become public officials, functionaries, and bureaucrats were based on Confucius's teachings and what came to be regarded as the spirit of those teachings. Confucianism, in this example, became what everybody knows and for that reason what everybody does in the many practical day-to-day decisions that have to be made in the life of an individual and a society. Decisions made in the middle-level structure or the surface structure, such as those regarding what kinds of festivals would be celebrated, whether divorce would be condoned, who would be educated and to what extent, and whether men and women would dine together, had to be congruent with the Confucian deep structure.

Having considered the concepts of deep structure and surface structure as they apply to a culture as a whole, we turn now to considering these same two concepts as they apply to the language of any given culture. In the analysis that follows we make use of the seminal and powerful ideas of the linguist Noam Chomsky, not necessarily because all linguists agree completely with his ideas but because they are particularly apt for showing how a knowledge of the deep structure of a culture's language leads to a knowledge of the deep structure of the culture itself.

Chomsky states that every language can be represented in such a way as to make clear the linguistic distinction between *surface structure* and *deep structure*, concepts we mentioned in a different context in chapter 2. He writes: " . . . let me introduce the term 'surface structure' to refer to a representation of the phrases that constitute a linguistic expression and the categories to which these phrases belong."[13] He continues: " . . . the further technical term 'deep structure' . . . refer[s] to a representation of the phrases that play a more central role in the semantic interpretation of a sentence."[14]

Chomsky states that: "What is important is . . . the view that deep structures which are often abstract exist and play a central role in the grammatical processes that we use in producing and interpreting sentences."[15] And: " . . . it is fair to conclude that surface structure determines phonetic form, and that the grammatical relations represented in deep structures are those that determine meaning."[16]

Setting the stage for our further analysis, Chomsky concludes:

> Such facts, then, support the hypothesis that deep structures of the sort postulated in transformational generative grammar are *real mental structures* [italics added]. These deep structures, along with the transformational rules that relate them to surface structure and the rules relating deep and surface structures to representation of sound and meaning, are the rules that have been mastered by the person who has learned a language. They constitute his knowledge of the language; they are put to use when he speaks and understands.[17]

Chomsky maintains that surface structure plays some role in determining semantic interpretation, but he adds that " . . . the surface structures give little indication of the semantic interpretation, whereas the deep structures are quite revealing in this respect."[18]

Chomsky's position, presented here in his own words, indicates the importance of the distinction between deep structure and surface structure in the study of linguistics. But the phenomenon suggested by his technical distinction and by the more or less scientific linguistic processes of discovering the deep structures or the real meaning of an expression is also a phenomenon of common everyday experience. Simply put, we often know what a sentence means even though the surface structure of the sentence does not necessarily provide an accurate indication of the deeper structures and relations on which the real meaning of the sentence depends. Linguistically, the surface structures of sentences can be very different from their deep structures.

Chomsky offers the following example to illustrate how we recognize the meaning of an English sentence even though that meaning is not accurately included in the sentence's surface structure: "John is certain to leave." The sentence in its surface structure merely attributes a given logical property (namely, the property of being certain) to the proposition that John will leave. Any person who knows English, however, realizes that the proposition "John will leave" expresses a part of the meaning of the sentence, although that proposition as such is not indicated in the sentence's surface structure. Chomsky goes on to say that to have acquired a knowledge of English grammar means precisely that a person has internalized the rules expressing the relations of deep and surface structure and the rules that relate paired deep and surface structures to phonetic representations on one hand and representations of meaning on the other. Such a person makes use of these internalized rules—totally without awareness or even the possibility of awareness—in producing the indefinite range of English sentences and in understanding sentences produced by others.

We can now ask the direct question: How does a knowledge of the deep structure of a culture's language lead to the learning and understanding of the deep structure of the culture itself? Another way of putting the same question is: Why does the culture learner who knows the language of the culture he is learning ordinarily have such a great learning advantage over the culture learner who does not?

These two questions might be answered at one level simply by pointing out that some of the key words and expressions in the deep structure of one culture cannot be adequately or appropriately translated into the language of another culture. In the example we used earlier, we saw that the Chinese word *jen,* which plays such an important role in the Confucian deep structure of Chinese culture, is one such word. Similarly, the Japanese word *kami* is not a good equivalent for the English word "God" or "Creator." Some expressions—"created equal," for example— that are well understood in one culture cannot be translated into another language at all because there is no corresponding concept in the thought patterns of the people who use that language. Other expressions, such as *sine qua non* and *habeas corpus,* are simply borrowed from Latin because there is no satisfactory way they can be rendered in English. Examples need not be multiplied. The phenomenon is well known to anyone who has attempted to translate from one language to another, although the naive assumption that other languages are just different words for the same thing dies hard.

The relationship between learning the deep structure of a language and learning the deep structure of a culture, however, is much more profound than just the matter of the degree to which words and ideas can be faithfully translated into other languages. Chomsky, as was already indicated, arrives at three conclusions about the relationships between deep structures and surface structure from a purely linguistic point of view: (1) that deep structures, though often quite abstract, exist and are real mental structures, (2) that each language has its own rules for relating deep structures to surface structure, and (3) that these rules are internalized and used both in producing sentences and in understanding them. Further study of each of these insights or conclusions will enable us to see more clearly how a knowledge of the language's deep structure leads to a better knowledge of the culture's deep structure.

## Mental Structures

It might at first seem almost trivial to say that one cannot know the meaning of a spoken or written sentence without knowing much more about it than the literal meaning of each of the words in the sentence. Interpreters, translators, and teachers of elementary language courses are especially aware of the fact that a sentence is more than the sum of the words it contains. Context, intonation, contrastive emphasis, and the like all play a part in establishing what the sentence means. But the hypothesis that deep structures are real mental structures, learned ways of detecting meaning, is far from trivial. What does the hypothesis mean?

It means basically that the deep structures of the sentences produced and understood in any language are functions of the mental sets, patterns, configurations—what we might call the logic—of the people who use that language. By extension, it means that to *think* in a particular language is to think in the way that the people, to whom that language is native, think. It means, for example, to know or sense what must be made explicit in order to be understood and what may be left unsaid without any fear of ambiguity or miscommunication. If the deep structures of a language are themselves real mental structures, however abstract, the culture learner who knows or is aware of these deep structures is already capable of thinking to some extent in the way the people of the culture think. This does not necessarily imply that he thinks *what* the people of the culture think in the sense of agreeing with their ideas and behaviors. But it does mean that some part of the mental structuring is the same. This is already close to the culture's deep structure.

Knowing the language, particularly the ability to recognize and understand the deep structure of the almost infinite variety of sentences produced within a culture, is therefore of immense value to the culture learner. It enables the culture learner to communicate, at the level of real meaning, with the people of that culture. More importantly, it makes it possible for him, as he tries to learn where the consensuses lie, to check and verify directly his own impressions as well as those of his sources of information.

## Rules

Linguists and grammarians have postulated that there are definite rules in every language for relating the deep and surface structures of sentences. What "the rules" in this case mean is that the deep and surface structures of sentences are not related in random, chance, or arbitrary ways. The rules prescribe what relationships are possible and what are not. A person who relates the deep structure and the surface structure of sentences in any way other than according to those rules will be producing ungrammatical or ambiguous sentences that fail to convey his message to those with whom he hopes to communicate. Chomsky summarizes as follows: "The generative grammar of a language specifies an infinite set of structural descriptions, each of which contains a deep structure, a surface structure, a phonetic representation, a semantic representation, and other formal structures. The rules relating deep and surface structure —the so-called 'grammatical transformation'—have been investigated in some detail, and are fairly well understood. The rules that relate surface structures and phonetic representation are also reasonably well understood (though I do not want to imply that the matter is beyond dispute; far from it)."[19]

Apart altogether from the truth value of any particular sentence, the rules relating deep to surface structure regulate both the grammaticality and the intelligibility or the meaning of the sentence. For example, the English sentence "John and Mary are married" can usually mean only that John and Mary are married to each other. Except under very special circumstances, English usage requires that a different construction be used if the speaker intends to convey the message that John is married to one person and Mary is married to another person. A person who has learned English well has internalized this rule— or this usage—in such a way that it never occurs to him to say "John and Mary are married" unless he means they are married to each other. Similarly, it would not occur to him to say "John and Mary are married to each other" because both he and the person to whom he is speaking would consider the phrase "to each other" redundant. Or another example: If a speaker of English says "John has lived in America," he clearly means that John is still living. If John were now dead, the speaker would have to say "John lived in America." Such a rule is simply recognized by both speaker and listener as part of correct English usage. And a third example: In the English sentence "John told Mary to come and see him," the word "him" clearly refers to John. Because of his knowledge of the rules relating deep to surface structure, the English-speaking person would not use this sentence if the word "him" referred to some person other than John.

These rules are usually very subtle and complex. The rules are learned or acquired in the course of learning and using the language; articulating them and demonstrating them logically or scientifically is quite another thing. They are not discovered by investigating introspectively either the individual psyche or the general nature of language. An English language speaker, for example, recognizes when he makes a grammatical mistake himself or when someone else does so, but this is a much different matter from trying to explain why it is a mistake, or what the rule is, or why the rule is as it is. As Chomsky puts it: "We use this knowledge [of the rules] totally without awareness or even the possibility of awareness, in producing these sentences or understanding them when they are produced by others."[20]

So important are the rules relating deep structure to surface structure in any language that the use of improper or incorrect grammar not only presents the possibility of misunderstanding, it makes misunderstanding all but inevitable. It may be true in certain verbal communications that it is not necessary to know and heed the grammatical rules for relating meaning (deep structure) to form (surface structure). We frequently hear people say that the grammatical form is not important as long as the other person understands the message. The fact is, however, that unless a person has learned the deep structure of a language as well as its surface structure, the message is as likely to be misunderstood and misinterpreted as it is to be understood. To use a former example, the person who says "John and Mary are married" when he means that John is married to one person and Mary to another is likely to leave his listener completely bewildered.

The task of establishing whether and how the transformational rules for any language arise and change is part of the field of linguistics. In an introduction to culture learning, it is sufficient to point out that there must also be rules, perhaps not as certain or ascertainable as those in linguistics, by which deep structure consensuses are transformed to surface consensuses in the culture generally. At the present stage of our speculation about such rules, this may mean little more than that there is always a consistency between deep structure opinions and values and their surface structure reflections. It can be safely assumed that no culture exists in which the people think, believe, and feel in one way and behave in ways that they find inconsistent with these thoughts and feelings. They may profess to believe something and behave in ways contrary to it, but this only means that they do not really believe and feel what they profess.

Thus, for example, if there is a deep structure consensus in a society that "all men are created equal," this deep structure consensus will be reflected, not only in such things as government, job opportunities, the administration of justice, and taxation but also in such things as forms of address, wearing apparel, and relationships between the sexes. To take another example: If there is a deep structure consensus in a culture that good or bad fortune in this life depends on one's moral conduct in an earlier life, this consensus will manifest itself in surface structure consensuses on areas ranging from abortion to senility. Furthermore, without being conscious of them, the culture will have worked out specific rules for determining which possible surface structure behaviors are in accord with the deep structure consensuses and which are not. Each culture will have its own rules, its own logic, for inferring from a deep structure consensus to a surface structure consensus—and vice versa—but no culture can be without some such rules.

It would be far too simple and naive to think that the path from deep structure consensus to surface structure consensus is in all cultures the direct path from principles (deep structure) to policies and then to practices (surface structure). In some cultures, for example, contradictions are allowed by the "rules" and in some cultures they are not. These "rules" will be quite different in a culture, for example, in which a main deep structure consensus is on harmonious relationships and one in which a main deep structure consensus is on the value of the truth, no matter how much it might do injury to harmonious interpersonal relationships.

### Internalization

Both language learning and culture learning involve a process of internalization, which means simply that the learner actualizes, appropriates, or makes his own what he sets out to learn. Internalization implies the newly acquired ability to function efficiently and effectively in the language or in the general culture itself. It implies further that this functioning is more or less natural, spontaneous, and effortless. In the case of language learning, the rules for transforming deep structures and surface structures are internalized when, in Chomsky's way of putting it, they are used without awareness or even the possibility of awareness in producing sentences or understanding sentences produced by others. Bilingual and trilingual persons have internalized a second or third language so thoroughly that it is impossible for the listener to tell which is the native or first language. When a language is internalized, thinking in that language becomes second nature.

The internalizing of another culture, through the process of culture learning, is inevitably a matter of greater or lesser degrees on a continuum. Toward one end of that continuum is the person who so fully internalizes a second culture that for all practical purposes he becomes a member of that culture. Its consensuses on opinion and behavior become his consensuses; its way of life becomes his way of life. Lafcadio Hearn, for example, may have approached this degree of internalization in his living among the Japanese. (Whether the Japanese people considered him a Japanese is a different matter.) Another well-known example is Albert Schweitzer in Africa.

Toward the other end of the continuum is the culture learner who has internalized enough of the culture's consensuses so that he can function reasonably well in the culture but neither he himself nor anyone else would consider him an expert on that culture. To use an analogy from language learning, he has begun to "think," feel, and empathize with that culture, but in many important ways it is still foreign to him and he to it. In fact, the internalization process in most culture learning stops short of the culture learner's coming to identify fully with that culture. A major first step in the process of internalizing the deep structure of another culture, however, is the learning of the language of that culture.

In this chapter we have argued that learning the language of a culture is the most important means or mode of culture learning but that it is not strictly indispensable to it. Some of the primary consensuses in a culture are nonverbal and analogic and are never stated in words. We have considered how language is a part of the very essence of a culture and how the deep and surface structures of the language greatly influence the deep and surface structures of the culture as a whole. We have stressed that the culture's language both reflects and determines the ways of thinking within a culture. As Cole and Scribner put it, " . . . consider the area of ideology or theoretical work in general, where concepts largely acquire their meanings through their being embedded in explanatory verbal networks. It is here that language may play the greatest role in shaping the person's view of reality, in influencing his memory and thinking processes, and in contributing to his understanding or misunderstanding of other cultures."[21] We turn next to view of reality or world view as one of the essential components of a culture and one of the central modes of culture learning.

## NOTES

1. The position taken here is that language is only a part of human communication and that much culture learning can take place through good translations. Those who insist that culture learning means understanding a culture in its own terms are likely to insist that one cannot learn a culture, that is, really know and understand that culture, without learning its language. The distinction between *emic* culture learning (learning a culture as those who are part of it perceive it), and *etic* culture learning (learning a culture from the outside or as part of a larger system), is frequently made in this connection. For an excellent brief analysis of this distinction see Richard W. Brislin, Walter J. Tonner, and Robert M. Thorndike, *Cross-Cultural Research Methods* (New York: John Wiley & Sons, 1973), pp. 24–25, 164–167.

2. Paul Watzlawick, Janet Helmick Beavin, and Don D. Jackson, *Pragmatics of Human Communication* (New York: W. W. Norton & Company, 1967), p. 63.

3. Edward Sapir, *Language, Culture and Personality, Essays in Memory of Edward Sapir,* as quoted by Benjamin Lee Whorf in *Language, Thought, and Reality,* ed. John B. Carroll (Cambridge, Mass.: The M.I.T. Press, 1956), p. 134.

4. Michael Cole and Sylvia Scribner, *Culture and Thought, A Psychological Introduction* (New York: John Wiley & Sons, 1974) p. 59.

5. Ibid., p. 60.

6. Whorf, *Language, Thought, and Reality,* pp. 147–148.

7. Ibid., p. 148.

8. Ibid., p. 151.

9. Ibid., p. 158.

10. Noam Chomsky, *Language and Mind* (New York: Harcourt Brace Jovanovich, 1972), ix.

11. Dun J. Li, *The Ageless Chinese,* 2nd ed. (New York: Charles Scribner's Sons, 1971), p. 74.

12. Ibid., p. 74.

13. Chomsky, *Language and Mind,* p. 105.

14. Ibid., p. 105.

15. Ibid., p. 107.

16. Ibid., p. 107.

17. Ibid., p. 107.

18. Ibid., p. 163.

19. Ibid., p. 110.

20. Ibid., p. 104.

21. Cole and Scribner, *Culture and Thought,* p. 59.

# chapter 5

# Cultural World Views

The purpose of this chapter is to explore the proposition that at the heart, the foundation, or the center of every culture there exists a consensus on a world view and that a large part of culture learning consists in discovering what this world view is and understanding what it means in the day-to-day life of the people of the culture. The basic idea of a world view is not in itself complicated. It simply means that the people of every culture have some explanation, some accounting, for the existence of the world and the universe in which they live and of which they feel a part. World view is concerned with final or ultimate explanations and is thus virtually the same as the culture's consensus on religious or philosophical questions.

World view can be said to begin where science ends; it is an attitude that seeks to supply answers to the questions that lie beyond the scope and power of empirical science. Those world views that are based on religion ordinarily involve some kind of a faith system in which doctrines are accepted and adhered to by reason of the presumed reliability of the source of that faith. World views, based on philosophical inquiry rather than religious faith, assume that the answers to ultimate questions can be at least partially uncovered through the use of human reason, usually in some form of metaphysical thinking and reasoning but sometimes as well in mystic experiencing. World views differ greatly in the degree to which they rely on scientific knowledge and seek to validate themselves scientifically, but their aim is always the wisdom that transcends science. The concept of a "scientific world view" would appear to be inherently contradictory because, among other things, such a world view would not be able to respond to the question of why science itself is a good or valuable thing. One of the main functions of a world view within a culture is to serve as a source and justifying reason for the culture's value system.

What do we mean when we say that every culture has and needs a consensus on world view? We mean nothing less than that each culture can continue in existence as a culture, that is, be identified and recognized as a culture, only so long as there is basic agreement within it on matters considered of ultimate importance. It is on the basis of this world view that the people of a culture determine what is and is not ultimately important in the organization of their common life and its institutions. A culture gains its vitality precisely from the fact that world view questions are not in serious dispute; if they were, the culture would soon fragment and disintegrate. In actual practice, those relatively few persons within a given culture who dissent from the culture's dominant world view are likely to be ostracized, excommunicated, imprisoned, or exiled for their lack of orthodoxy. Even cultures that are most open, free and individualistic, that is, cultures with a broad tolerance for dissent on fundamental issues, must safeguard themselves against world views or ideologies that themselves do not tolerate freedom for others.

Apart from the more important fact that cultures cannot function as cultures without a consensus on world view that serves as the ultimate source and explanation of values, different cultures arrive at different world views as a way of satisfying natural intellectual curiosity about such matters. World view probably comes most often to the consciousness of the adults in a culture when they are asked by their innocently inquisitive children to answer such questions as, "Why was I born me rather than someone else?" or "Where did the stars come from?" or "Who made God?"

Before considering briefly the origin, nature, and kinds of world views, it should be pointed out that world views are at first accepted uncritically and unquestioningly by most members of the culture. The process of accepting a world view begins at birth and perhaps even earlier. As part of the traditional wisdom, world views are handed down from generation to generation, from parents to children, in the ordinary process of nurture and education. In a devout Christian family, for example, children will begin to learn their prayers as early as they begin to learn their ABCs; the earliest stories they hear are likely to be Bible stories. At this early age, children accept whatever answers are given as *the* answers. Children usually have trust and confidence in those who are taking care of them and, even when this is not the case, children have no choice but to allow their thinking and feeling to be shaped by those with whom they are in close contact.

It should also be noted that questions concerning a culture's world view, whether they are posed by the young, the adults, or the aging, will differ from culture to culture because the world view itself determines what questions can and cannot arise. Certain questions that arise in one culture never enter the consciousness of persons in other cultures.

Then, too, a world view is simply received and respected by most of the people in a given culture because they see no need to question it and because they might not have the time or the inclination or the education necessary to question it even if they did. Most people are far too preoccupied with the immediate concerns and problems of everyday life to give much serious attention to the remoter problems of their own world view. Furthermore, most people in a culture will have absorbed the world view of their culture at such an early age that their main effort—when questions of the world view's nature and validity do arise—is to defend and legitimate that world view rather than to question its fundamental premises and presuppositions. Interestingly, even in college years, when students are taught that the "unexamined life is not worth living," few take seriously the challenges to the particular world view that they earlier accepted in an unexamined way.

We introduced earlier the distinction between vertical and horizontal cultures, that is, between those that tend to stay within some kind of geographical or national limitations and those that cut across such boundaries. Here we must explore that distinction somewhat more fully. Buddhist, Islamic, and Christian cultures, for example, have long been recognized as horizontal cultures because they are not restricted to national boundaries. Marxian economic determinism, however, has given a new importance to the distinction between vertical and horizontal cultures in the modern world.

We have seen that, according to Marx, class consciousness shapes and determines all modern world views—or at least those that make any difference. We also noted that in Marx's view the poor, the rich, the industrial workers, the bourgeoisie, and the tenant farmers of one country have the same world view as the equivalent classes of other countries. Marx's challenge has been strongly felt throughout the world because he would have those who are seeking to understand the world views of others ask not what nation they belong to but what class they belong to. Marx insisted that the class struggle is the only vital world view and that the class struggle consists essentially in the rich trying to maintain the *status quo*, and along with it their wealth and privilege, and the poor trying to overturn the *status quo*.[1]

An introduction to culture learning is not the place to consider economic determinism, Marxian or any other kind, in detail. What is necessary to understand, however, is that in economic determinism and dialectical materialism as synthesizing world views Marx felt he had found the corrective to all other more particularistic world views. Marx saw religious world views as false hopes held out to the masses to prevent them from revolting. He saw world views based on concepts of harmony, cooperation, compassion, and altruism as ideological superstructures intended to keep those who are without economic power from recognizing the desperateness of their lot. In short, he saw all metaphysical positions, except his own, merely as devices for postponing the inevitable class warfare that would eventually result in a completely classless world society.

It would also take us too far ahead here to attempt to make any judgments about how the older and newer nationalisms will ultimately fare as vertical cultures in competition with Marxist-Leninist doctrines. Recent events tend to indicate that the Communist Party, in Russia and China as well as in other countries, has had to make accommodations to the powerful and basic loyalties, traditions, and world views of the vertical (nationalist) cultures. In short, although Marx has opened up important new research concerns for culture learning, it would seem that economic determinism is far too narrow a concept either to explain the origin of world views among cultures or to serve as the exclusive world view for any particular culture. Man is an economic animal, but he is also more than that; cultures in turn draw on much more than their economic life and condition in arriving at their consensuses on world view.

## The Origin of World Views

As indicated earlier, a world view is the attempt by the people of a culture to answer certain fundamental questions about the nature of the world and about man's place and purposes, if any, in it. The consensus within a culture about how these questions can and should best be answered usually results in an organic and dynamic way from the teachings and way of life of certain persons who are considered particularly wise, inspired, effective, or responsible. The teaching and example of these persons become in the course of generations the accepted opinions and behaviors of the culture as a whole. These persons become the authorities and the criteria for the world views that are then simply received by subsequent generations.

The world view deals ultimately with the mysterious, inexplicable, and ineffable, but it is the culture's way of comprehending and explaining things in the world and things that happen in the world. World views are sometimes said to be either *ontological,* because they emphasize answers to the question, "Why is there something rather than nothing at all?" or *cosmological,* because they stress the answers to the question, "What kinds of things are there?"

Great teachers, seers, sages, and saints are among the "heroes" in any culture. They perceive the inadequacy of the culture's earlier world view and seek to replace it in whole or in part. Sometimes their knowledge and power is viewed as coming from some secret, hidden, or supernatural source; other times as coming from enlightenment, depth of feeling, and clarity of insight. Always they arrive on the scene when the consensuses are breaking down and the people are more or less ready for new ideas and new directions. As Joseph Campbell has pointed out, these teachers or heroes may regard themselves as teaching their own people or they may regard themselves as teaching all mankind. "Tribal or local heroes, such as the emperor Huang Ti, Moses, or the Aztec Texcallipoca, commit their boons to a single folk; universal heroes—Mohammed, Jesus, Gautama Buddha—bring a message for the entire world."[2]

Even in an age of science, world views are based on assumptions and hypotheses. In more primitive societies, world views are based on the mythologies that have come to be regarded as authoritative explanations which, if they cannot be proved, either are not questioned or at least cannot be disproved. The questions which the world view seeks to answer are so vast, complex, and hidden that the expounders of world views necessarily call on parables, analogies, personifications, and dramatic episodes to make their world view as clear and meaningful as possible. World views, however, are no less meaningful to those who hold them and believe in them by reason of the fact that they are mythological and anthropocentric. For many, the mythological is just as real and convincing as so-called scientific explanations might be for others. The prevailing world view in a culture must work, must serve its purpose, but it need not be true and indeed cannot be true in any compelling objective sense.

Joseph Campbell makes the following summary statement about mythology:

> Mythology has been interpreted by the modern intellect as a primitive, fumbling effort to explain the world of nature (Frazer); as a production of poetical fantasy from prehistoric times, misunderstood by succeeding ages (Miller); as a repository of allegorical instruction, to shape the individual to his group (Durkheim); as a group dream, symptomatic of archetypal urges within the depths of the human psyche (Jung); as the traditional vehicle of man's profoundest metaphysical insights (Coomaraswamy); and as God's Revelation to His children (the Church). Mythology is all of these. The various judgments are determined by the view-points of the judges. For when scrutinized in terms not of what it is but of how it functions, of how it

has served mankind in the past, of how it may serve today, mythology shows itself to be as amenable as life itself to the obsessions and requirements of the individual, the race, the age.[3]

Various authors[4] have attempted to demonstrate that changes in world views follow a normal and predictable pattern from the more imaginary and mythological, to the religious and philosophical, and then to a third and final stage, the scientific. They point out that world views have their beginnings in whatever explanations and interpretations seem to work—however fanciful they may seem to others to be—but that the force of science, with its demand for verifiability and its insistence on critical doubt, eventually replaces world views that cannot withstand scientific scrutiny. This position has led to an immense amount of confusion for two reasons: (1) As already mentioned, the very idea of a scientific world view is inherently contradictory. The world view attempts to account for those phenomena which are beyond the reach of science, that is, precisely those phenomena which are not publicly verifiable. (2) World views that attempt to be scientific or to validate themselves scientifically become in fact "world hypotheses" rather than world views. Stephen C. Pepper in his excellent book, *World Hypotheses,* makes clear that no one of the major world hypotheses is adequate and that the only tenable position is one of "rational clarity in theory and reasonable eclecticism in practice."[5] According to Pepper, formism, mechanism, contextualism, and organicism are all equally valid though competing hypotheses or "views," even at the level of science.

The actual living world view, composed of the common beliefs and standards in a culture as explained and legitimated by the people who are formed and informed by it, is gradually developed and unfolded. It is all that people coherently believe to be right and excellent within their culture. It is, as Michael Polanyi writes, a kind of crystallization of the " . . . utterances of prophets, poets, legislators, scientists and other masters, or the messages of men who, by their actions, recorded in history, have set a pattern for posterity."[6]

Huston Smith wrote that "the surest way to the heart of a people is through their religion, assuming it is still alive and has not fossilized."[7] It would be at least equally correct to say that the surest way to the heart and mind of a people is through their consensus on a world view. Whether it be a religious world view or not, some world view is always active in a culture. One world view may replace another in the course of time, but by definition every culture has a consensus on world view at all times. Thus, for example, even the view that the world as such is utterly incomprehensible is a world view.

## Nature of World Views

World views, whatever their specific content or substance may be, have their origin in man's deep psychological desire to be able to explain and find meanings, that is, to discover causes and to understand interrelationships. Man finds himself in a world in which knowledge and wisdom are power; a world, moreover, in which to be without some principle or principles by which the events, activities, occurrences, and happenings of daily life can be structured is to be bewildered and disoriented. The world view is the response of intelligence in its encounter with the world and the fact of conscious experience; it both springs from interpretations and explanations that have been found satisfactory in the past and sets the limits to possible interpretations of the future. The world view fulfills an integrating function in individual and group thinking and behaving. It is the culture's way of specifying purposes and determining priorities, whether these are seen as subjective and created by the culture or as imposed by some natural or transcended order. Finally, the world view is the basis of organization, consistency, and stability within the culture and as such becomes the ultimate referent for decision making in the life of the culture.

Every world view takes into account and seeks to explain (1) the world of nature, (2) the world of fellow man, (3) the world of the self.

The world view of any particular culture offers the members of that culture an explanation of how the natural world came to be as it is, of what things in nature are supportive of man and his efforts and those that may well destroy him, of what things are good and to be enjoyed and those that are to be feared, dreaded, and avoided at all costs. Especially, the world view attempts to make clear whether man himself is a part of nature or whether nature exists not only as man's habitat but also for man's sake and purposes. Do, for example, horses and carabao exist so that men can ride them and use them to plow his field, or is man's control over these animals completely fortuitous? Or, as a more aesthetic example, do the beauties of a sunset, a waterfall, or a seascape exist to delight the soul of man or are these beauties simply the result of man's having developed within himself a capacity to react in certain ways to what he meets in nature?

When we say that the world view seeks to explain the world of nature—fire, water, air, earth, trees, sun, moon, stars, thunder, lightning and all such things—we do not exclude what is commonly called the supernatural. World views that incorporate a supernatural component usually do not regard this component, whatever its form, as unnatural or contrary to nature. Rather, the supernatural is seen as a higher order of reality than that immediately accessible through the senses.

That part of the culture's world view that seeks to explain what nature is will be decisive in determining what man's relationship to nature should be. Everything from whether the people are vegetarians to how they view environmental protection and the conservation of endangered species will depend on the consensus within the culture about what nature is and to what uses it should or should not be put. Of basic importance in every culture and every age, questions of man's relationship with nature have become crucial in the modern age because, for example, the birth rate worldwide is increasing so rapidly, the human lifespan is being extended, and the depletion rate of nonrenewable natural resources has so greatly accelerated.

A second essential part of a culture's world view attempts to answer questions of what man's relationship with his fellow men should be. Another way of putting it is that man's relationships with his fellow men will depend on how his world view leads him to perceive other human beings. If, for example, in a particular culture's world view the human being is seen as possessing inherent dignity, existing in an entirely different order of being than other animals, this perception will inevitably be reflected in the culture's teachings and actions with regard to human interrelationships. If, on the other hand, man is seen as simply a higher form of animal life, this perception will result in practicing a different kind of social relationships. Or again, if man is viewed as free, relatively independent, and individualistic, social relationships will take certain forms. If fellow men are seen as predators and competitors, social relationships will reflect wariness, distrust, and distance; if fellow men are seen as friendly and cooperative, social relationships will take on much more mutual trust and sharing. If human beings are viewed as objects, things, numbers—rather than as persons—social relationships will be correspondingly lacking in sensitivity, fellow feeling, and intersubjectivity.

Freud expresses his ideas of how thinking about the proper relationships between and among human beings come to be an integral part of any world view in *Civilization and Its Discontents.* According to Freud, " . . . what decides the purpose of life is simply the program of the pleasure principle."[8] He goes on to say:

> The last, but certainly not the least important, of the characteristic features of civilization remains to be assessed: the manner in which the relationships of men to one another are regulated—relationships which affect a person as a neighbor, as a source of help, as another person's sexual object, as a member of a family and of a State. Here it is especially difficult to keep clear of particular ideal demands and to see what is civilized in general . . . this replacement of the power of the individual by the power of a community constitutes the decisive step of civilization . . . the first requisite of civilization, therefore, is justice . . . [9]

Different cultures with different world views will, as Freud points out, base their concepts of what relationships of men to one another should be on different ideals—compassion, love, harmony, mutual respect, responsibility, and the like—but each culture will also have at its very core its own consensus on a concept of fundamental justice and fairness.

A third part of every world view involves some concept of the *self,* the individual person. This is also the case with the culture's thinking about the things of nature and social relationships, so that thinking about the self both forms and is informed by the culture's world view. The self is the domain of the introspective, the subjective, the experiencing. It is, if we may put it this way, the relationship of the self to the self, that is, each person's private intellectual and emotional sphere into which no one else can enter. It is the "I" or the "ego" that in some real sense constructs its own world of realities and visions, of memory and imagination, of hopes, fears, ambitions, and desires. The self is the person alone, in solitude, unique, private.

It is the culture as a whole and particularly its world view that shapes, molds, and fashions the self and the self's concept of itself. In some cultures every effort is made, as it were, to annihilate the self by bringing the self into conformity with the more or less standardized selves of the group as a whole. In other cultures the self is encouraged to grow and expand and to express itself in its own way. Some cultures regard the self and the soul (or the spirit) as the same, and they see in the self the powers of purification, salvation, reincarnation, transmigration and, in general, self-determination. Other cultures perceive the self as a biological organism that simply and in some still unknown way has achieved a higher consciousness than other forms of biological organisms. Whatever the world view, culture may be said to be embodied in all of the individual selves that make it up.

A culture's world view can be understood as the sum total of its thinking about nature, fellow man, and self. All three components will be found to be present to a greater or lesser extent in every world view. Nonetheless, some cultures tend to emphasize one component over the others, and within cultures these emphases tend to remain relatively stable and consistent.

Western cultures by and large have emphasized man's relationships to nature—or, more correctly, one particular aspect of that relationship. The Judeo-Christian tradition, so heavily influenced by Greek thought, has seen man as something radically distinct, as being of a different order than what is called lower nature. Man is essentially above the rest of nature and nature exists for man, with both man and nature existing by reason of their having been created by God. Whatever exists in nature, according to this view, is at man's disposal to be used in such a way as to help him attain his own higher objectives. Those forces in nature that are benevolent can be used to man's advantage and those forces that are malevolent are to be tamed, subdued, and controlled to whatever extent possible. The great impetus of Western science and technology in the modern era has been to make nature even more responsive and yielding to man's needs. Western man has felt the need to know more and more about the laws of nature and the natural law, but his viewpoint has been that of one who stands outside of nature rather than that of one who stands within it as a part of a larger whole. Traditionally, Western man has seen himself as called by his own nature to a higher life, an ultimate destiny of union with God, of which none of the lower forms of nature is capable.[10]

Similarly, the cultures that derive from and comprise traditional Chinese civilization have tended to put highest emphasis in their world views on social relationships, that is, on the relationship of human beings to one another. Their world view is such that harmonious relationships among human beings is of utmost value because on these everything else depends. Confucius based his philosophy on the concept that there are certain rights and responsibilities that result from established relationships among people—for example, ruler to people, father to son, and brother to brother—and that as long as these are properly respected and observed, everything else may be expected to take care of itself. Shame and the loss of face resulted only from someone's having disrupted the harmony that should prevail in all social relationships throughout the social order.

In Indian civilization, the world view has tended to emphasize the centrality of the *self*. Knowing oneself and mastering, disciplining, and controlling oneself is the way to inner peace and ultimately to enlightenment and Nirvana.

Buddha lived all his life in India. Buddhism has developed along several different lines, but David J. Kalupahana, a leading contemporary student of Buddhism, points out that in Buddhist philosophy "the noblest happiness . . . is to be achieved through the control of all hankering for the world [of sense pleasures], all coveting of false values, together with the dejection to which their impermanence and lack of enduring satisfaction give rise.

This is achieved through right, complete, and perfect mindfulness."[11] Kalupahana goes on to say that perfect mindfulness involves contemplating body in the body, feeling in the feelings, consciousness in the consciousness. Perfect mindfulness is consequently the way to detachment and purification.

Huston Smith, in his analysis of Hinduism, India's principal religion, describes the Indian cultural emphasis on the self in a way that is somewhat more comprehensible to persons of Western culture. He writes:

> All of us dwell on the brink of the infinite ocean of life's creative power. We all carry it within us; supreme strength, the fullness of wisdom, unquenchable joy. It is never thwarted and cannot be destroyed. But it is hidden deep, which makes life a problem. The infinite is down in the darkest, profoundest vault of our being, in the forgotten well-house, the deep cistern. What if we could discover it again and draw from it unceasingly?
> This question became India's obsession.[12]

We have seen that world views are made up of attitudes and opinions, consensuses about nature, fellow man, and self. We have also seen that historically, cultures have tended in their world views to stress one of these elements more fully than the others.

Freud sees the world view itself and the emphasis different cultures place in their world views on nature, the social group, or the self as the culture's way of overcoming what it perceives to be either its best opportunity or the dominant threat to its survival. Both the opportunity and the threat arise out of the clash between the pleasure principle and the repressions and restraints necessarily imposed on individuals by the society. Freud states "No feature, however, seems better to characterize civilization than its esteem and encouragement of man's higher mental activities—his intellectual, scientific and artistic achievements—and the leading role that it assigns to ideas in human life. Foremost among these ideas are the religious systems. . . . Next come the speculations of philosophy; and finally what might be called man's 'ideals'—his ideas of a possible perfection of individuals, or of peoples or of the whole of humanity, and the demands he sets up on the basis of such ideas."[13] The world views of different cultures emphasize nature, the social group, or the self depending on how their ideas and ideals lead them to define the perfection of individuals, cultures, and humanity in general.

Freud, perhaps more fully than anyone before him, was aware that culture mediates between man and man's perception of the real. Freud goes on to explain that not only will the world view of each culture show a tendency to emphasize fellow men, the self, or nature but also that, within each culture, individuals will show the same tendency to emphasize one or the other. According to Freud, "In this, [man's] psychical constitution will play a decisive role, irrespectively of the external circumstances. The man who is predominantly erotic will give first preference to his emotional relationships to other people; the narcissistic man, who inclines to be self-sufficient, will seek his main satisfaction in his internal mental processes; the man of action will never give up the external world on which he can try out his strength."[14]

## Kinds of World Views

This section might also be called *views* of world views. We have already seen that each person has a more or less well-articulated world view, that is, some sense or feeling of what the world is and what is or is not important in the world. Except in the case of rare creative geniuses, the world view held by individual persons will be much the same as that held by the other people in the same culture; most individuals simply accept and share in the consensus on world view that obtains in their culture. Furthermore, there is no way that anyone can see, examine, or investigate other world views except in the perspective provided by his own world view. When it comes to examining world views as a whole or even distinguishing among the kinds of world views that have or do exist, investigators use the categories and the classifying system that they know and think most appropriate. Investigators from other cultures would no doubt use other categories in distinguishing among the world's many different world views. Freud makes the point, so essential to culture learning, in this way:

It seems certain that we do not feel comfortable in our present-day civilization, but it is difficult to form an opinion whether and in what degree men of an earlier age felt happier and what part their cultural conditions played in the matter. We shall always tend to consider people's distress objectively—that is, to place ourselves, with our wants and sensibilities, in *their* conditions, and then to examine what occasions we should find in them for experiencing happiness or unhappiness. This method of looking at things, which seems objective because it ignores the variations in subjective sensibility, is of course the most subjective possible, since it puts one's own mental states in place of any others, unknown though they may be.[15]

An introduction to culture learning is not the place to attempt to make an exhaustive list or typology of real and possible world views. But it is important to know some of the ways the many different kinds of world views might be classified or distinguished one from the other.

World views might be classified according to their position on a rationalist-romanticist continuum. This means that world views can be differentiated according to whether they are based more on human reason and experience or more on feelings, hopes, aspirations, and utopian constructs. In the classical expression, the former tend to be more tough minded and the latter more tender minded. Another way of classifying the different kinds of world views is best expressed in the distinction between those cultures that see reality as immediately apprehended, intuitive, and aesthetic and those that see reality as logically and scientifically deduced and indirectly verified. A third way of classifying the kinds of world views is according to whether they conceive of the world (universe) as finite or infinite, and as monistic, dualistic, or pluralistic. Classifications of this type highlight the comprehensiveness of world views and make clear that every problem of culture, knowledge, or life itself is grounded ultimately in some kind of a world view. A fourth way of classifying world views, closely related to the third, would be according to how the world view deals with space and time, process and change, appearance and reality. A fifth way of classifying world views, as well as entire cultures, is based on their tendency to be either sacred or secular. Finally, although this list is not intended to be exhaustive, world views are sometimes classified for certain purposes as simply traditional, transitional, or modern.

## Two Contrasting World Views

We have examined briefly the concept of world view and we have seen how fundamental the understanding of a culture's world view is to learning that culture. This section attempts to illustrate and highlight the vast differences among contemporary world views. It does so by a general contrasting of two world views that are in almost every particular as different as they could possibly be. Each of the world views contrasted here represents only a small percentage of the world's population. Other world views that could be contrasted would have vastly larger numbers of adherents. But each of these two worlds views—one relatively simple and the other relatively complex— will tell us something of importance about the nature of world views.

The first is the world view of the Kpelle, a culture of approximately 150,000 people. These people speak a Mande language and live in Liberia, Africa. Research on the Kpelle has been particularly rich and insightful.

John Gay and Michael Cole lived among the Kpelle over an extended period of time and studied them thoroughly. They report that the world view of the Kpelle is especially interesting because their world is almost literally *the* world. According to Gay and Cole, for the Kpelle "knowledge is the ability to demonstrate one's mastery of the Kpelle way of life. Truth is the conformity of one's statements and actions to that way of life."[16] As understood by Gay and Cole, the Kpelle do not recognize any ultimate standards; they feel that their culture is its own reason for existence; they hold that truths are self-validating. "Yesterday's statement of a given truth is the justification for today's statement of it and for tomorrow's action based on it . . . It is not so much 'What is, is right' as 'What has been, is right.' "[17]

Kpelle children who go off to school, where they might learn new ideas and values, are regarded as having left the tribe. Of their own choice they have joined some new tribe, even though they still call themselves Kpelle. Of education within the tribe itself, Gay and Cole write:

Knowledge for its own sake seems to have no place in Kpelle society. Education fashions the child in the mold of his ancestors. He learns to do what his parents and the village and the tribe and the history of his people force him to do. Knowledge as a preservative of the community, and as a support for the prestige of the elders, has great value. Education perpetuates a way of life and so produces a reverence for what has been. It stifles individual creativity that the system might survive.[18]

The second world view, in stark contrast with that of the Kpelle, is the world view of those philosophers, artists, and scientists who see a transnational, transcultural world view as already in the process of emerging. These people come together from a large number of vertical (national or geographic) cultures to form what we have earlier identified as a horizontal culture. Generally speaking, this is a network of people found planning and running international and intercultural organizations, carrying on research across national boundaries, writing for international periodicals, and participating in international conferences, seminars, and workshops. Their works are well known to one another if not always as yet to the general public.

Julian Huxley, former Director General of UNESCO, whose search for a "common background of thought"[19] was mentioned earlier, was one such person. Another is F. S. C. Northrop. His pioneering book, *The Meeting of East and West,* is a profound and eloquent statement of what he sees as an emerging world view that correlates the best in Eastern and Western cultures without in any way diminishing either.

Northrop maintains that all world views can ultimately be traced to either of two fundamentally different but complementary ways of knowing. For Northrop, all concepts and all knowing are based on (1) intuition and (2) postulation. He feels it can be demonstrated that the cultures of the East use concepts by intuition as their primary way of knowing and that the cultures of the West use concepts by postulation as their primary way of knowing. Concepts by intuition are those that comprise the aesthetic component; the complete meaning of the concept is given by something immediately apprehended. " 'Blue' in the sense of the sensed color is an example of a concept by intuition."[20] Concepts by postulation are those whose meaning may

be proposed for them postulationally in some specific deduc-
tively formulated theory. " 'Blue' in the sense of the number for
the wavelength for light in experimentally confirmed, deductive-
ly formulated electromagnetic theory is an example of a concept
by postulation."[21]

Northrop is thus able to summarize his idea of a synthesizing
universal world view in one paragraph:

> By the same token, when the relation of epistemic correlations
> joins concepts by intuition which are particulars to concepts by
> postulation which are universals, and when it requires both types of
> concepts to refer to two factors in the nature of all things which are
> both real, ultimate, and meaningful, it indicates each of the diverse
> modern, medieval, Eastern and Western cultures to be giving expres-
> sions to something which is in part true, and it shows precisely how
> to relate and reconcile them all without conflict or contradiction so
> that a peaceful comprehensive world civilization approximating more
> closely to the expression of the whole truth is possible.[22]

Writing in a somewhat more popular view, Carl Sagan, scientist and newspaper columnist, offers another explanation of this
emerging world view. He compares the exploration of outer
space to the terrestrial explorations of Marco Polo and Magellan.
Just as these explanations opened vistas, broadened possibilities,
and provided profound new perspectives to a relatively ingrown
and insular Europe, so "it is possible to see how planetary exploration is already beginning a deprovincialization of Earth."[23]
The explorations of Marco Polo and Magellan opened the eyes
of Europeans to the fact that there were other lands, other
peoples, other ways of viewing the world. Sagan sees a similarity
in the circumstances, then and now. He states:

> Our planet has been explored. We are in the midst of a great cultural
> and technological homogenization, in which common habits of
> thought and a shared world view are rapidly embracing even the most
> distant and obscure parts of our small planet. At just this moment
> comes an opportunity to examine other worlds, neighboring planets
> in space which are in some ways similar and in some ways profoundly
> different from our familiar world.[24]

Sagan maintains that the Space Age and Space Age exploration force us to develop new perspectives, new world views, new habits of thought, new values. He says: "By examining other worlds we have a significant chance of improving our understanding of nature, of the origin and fate of our planet and ourselves."[25]

And John W. Gardner, founder of Common Cause, sees still another reason behind the emerging of a new and global world view: the growing consciousness of our shared responsibility for our small planet, Spaceship Earth. He writes: "Our planet is but a speck of dust, and our life on it is but an instant in the long stretch of astrophysical time. Still, it is the only planet we have and our life on it holds great possibilities of beauty, dignity and meaning. Yet if it were asked of us how we spend our time on our speck of dust, we would have to say, 'We spend a good deal of it fighting one another and laying waste to our earth.' "[26]

Gardner goes on to assert that every modern nation is a composite of earlier tribalisms and fierce regional loyalties that have given way—or are almost sure to give way eventually—to national identity. And, he concludes, "it is not inconceivable that the same process might occur world-wide. In any case, it is only out of respect for our common humanity that we can create the sense of relatedness and mutuality that will prevent this riven, angry, frightened world from tearing itself to pieces."[27]

This very sketchy juxtaposing and contrasting of the Kpelle world view with what might be called an emerging global world view has been for the purpose of illustrating how completely world views can and do differ from one another. Value judgments about either or both world views are not relevant to the making of that point. The important conclusion to be drawn from the illustration and this chapter as a whole is that the world view is a culture's essence. One might go further and say that culture learning is essentially the apprehending of the culture's world view. This culture's many less basic and less comprehensive consensuses on opinion and behavior will be found to be rooted or implicated in that world view.

A culture's concept of the law, while part of its deep structure, is among those consensuses derived from its world view. It is to the law as a means of culture learning that we turn next.

NOTES

1. For a thorough analysis of the Marxian position, see Karl Mannheim, *Ideology and Utopia; An Introduction to the Sociology of Knowledge,* trans. Louis Wirth and Edward Shils, (London: K. Paul, Trench, Trubner and Co., 1936), p. 318.

2. Joseph Campbell, *The Hero with a Thousand Faces* (New York: Pantheon Books, 1949), p. 38.

3. Ibid., p. 38.

4. See, for example, August Comte's *System of Positive Polity* (Paris: L. Mathias, 1851–55).

5. Stephen C. Pepper, *World Hypotheses* (Berkeley: University of California Press, 1957), p. 330.

6. Michael Polanyi, *Personal Knowledge* (Chicago: University of Chicago Press, 1962), p. 375.

7. Huston Smith, *The Religions of Man* (New York: Mentor Books, 1958), p. 19.

8. Sigmund Freud, *Civilization and Its Discontents,* ed. and trans. James Strachey (New York: W. W. Norton & Company, 1961), p. 23.

9. Ibid., p. 42.

10. "Traditionally" needs to be stressed here. In fact, the Western world is in the process of undergoing a profound secularization in which many of the traditional concepts and values are being modified and changed. The vestiges of earlier world views are nonetheless still profoundly felt. The theologian Bernard Haring writes: " . . . we must remember that the process of secularization is not affirmed with the same depth or emphasis in all contemporary human groupings. In certain areas, the process is barely beginning, as in Africa and parts of Asia, while in others it is firmly implanted, as in North America, northern and western Europe." *Faith and Morality in the Secular Age* (Garden City, N.Y.: Doubleday, 1973), p. 23.

11. David J. Kalupahana, *Buddhist Philosophy: A Historical Analysis* (Honolulu: The University Press of Hawaii, 1976), p. 61.

12. Smith, *Religions,* p. 39.

13. Freud, *Civilization and Its Discontents,* p. 41.

14. Ibid., p. 30.

15. Ibid., p. 36.

16. John Gay and Michael Cole, *The New Mathematics and an Old Culture: A Study of Learning among the Kpelle of Liberia* (New York: Holt, Rinehart and Winston, 1967), p. 89.

17. Ibid., p. 90.

18. Ibid., p. 90.

19. See Julian Huxley, *UNESCO: Its Purposes and Its Philosophy* (Washington, D.C.: Public Affairs Press, 1948), p. 46.

20. F. S. C. Northrop, *The Meeting of East and West* (New York: The Macmillan Company, 1946), p. 448.

21. Ibid., p. 448.

22. Ibid., p. 449.

23. Carl Sagan, "Ships Sailing in Cosmic Seas," in the Honolulu *Advertiser*, August 1, 1976, p. B-6.

24. Ibid., p. B-1.

25. Ibid., p. B-6.

26. John W. Gardner, "A Broad Look at the Modern World," *Aspen Institute Quarterly* 9 (1976): 2.

27. Ibid., p. 2.

*chapter* 6
# The Rule of Law

The law is that way found in every country or culture for promoting justice and controlling the behavior of human beings in their relationships to other persons and to institutions. Just as every culture has some form of world view, so every culture has some form of legal system; the two are very closely interrelated. The legal system may be relatively simple and so taken for granted that it can hardly be distinguished from the mores, customs, and folkways of the people. Or it may be elaborately structured and highly formalized, requiring the full-time work of specially educated people to make, interpret, and enforce the law.

Studying the law and the legal system that prevails within a culture, together with the attitudes of the people toward the law, can be the source of some of the profoundest insights in the whole of culture learning. Although it is probably true that most of the people in every culture never find it necessary to step inside a courtroom, the legal system as such extends into practically every aspect of their lives. This is especially true in the modern world. As C. G. Weeramantry points out: "The tasks placed upon the law by the present age grow enormously from year to year. An ever-widening segment of the individual's life is encompassed by law and legal regulation. Tax laws, highway codes, hire-purchase acts, rating laws, town and country planning acts, social security regulations, legal aid rules and administrative decisions crowd in upon his life, bringing him in daily contact with the law in a manner unknown before."[1]

## Legal Theory

To understand the importance of law as a means or a mode of culture learning, it is first necessary to understand something of legal theory or the concept of law. The first thing to note is that *law* is a very comprehensive term. It is not essential here to go into the various levels of law or the various kinds of law, except to point out that in this discussion we are not at all concerned with what are called the "laws of nature" or the laws of the physical world. The idea of law as a social force or institution is the essential point, and the distinction commonly made between the *rule of law* and the *rules of law* is immensely helpful in understanding this idea.

The difference between the two terms is that *rule of law* refers to the commitment of the members of a society to call upon human reason and historical experience for the ordering of their society. This term suggests that there are certain jural postulates, that is, public perspectives and attitudes that, taken together, virtually define for the society what is just, fair, equitable, and consequently either *lawful* or *unlawful*. The *rule of law* is thus the antithesis of both the rule of arbitrary power and force and of anarchy. *Rules of law,* on the other hand, are simply those specific customary or statutory regulations by means of which the rule of law is made functional in different societies. The *rule of law* is basic and changes, if at all, only very slowly. The *rules of law,* specifying what is to be done and what is to be avoided, change much more rapidly as new social conditions make such changes or additions necessary.

Implicit in the distinction between *rule of law* and *rules of law* is the idea that *rule of law* is always legitimate while *rules of law* may or may not be so. No society—even the smallest or the most rudimentary—can exist without law; the historical record confirms the familiar saying that "wherever there is society, there is law." The *rule of law* is closely allied to the concept that law is desirable, if not absolutely necessary, in human affairs and that development of the law and the state of orderly relationships among individuals and among groups that is known as civilization were concurrent phenomena. The *rules of law*, however, may be the edicts, decrees, and dictates of tyrants and usurpers as well as the legitimate prescriptions and proscriptions of valid governments. No government can govern without laying down rules which at least temporarily and in the practical order have the force of law, because those who are governed have no viable choice other than to obey them. Specific *rules of law*, while in theory formulated to promote the achieving of justice, may in practice actually thwart that objective.

What, then, is the law as distinguished from the actual laws, whether written or unwritten? Palmer D. Edmunds, without precisely defining the law, gives an excellent brief description of it:

> Out of the raw material of the nation, which is merely a community conscious of its own unity, individuality and will to endure as a distinctive geographical, linguistic and cultural unit, men fashion the body politic, a society rationally organized for the purpose of establishing, maintaining and perfecting the conditions necessary and appropriate for community life to perform its role in the complete development of man. For the most part, these conditions consist in the maintenance of external peace and order, the protection of personal liberty, the regulation of property and commerce in the common interest, and the just settlement of conflicting claims.[2]

The law, as Palmer states, is the society's way of rationally organizing itself for the purpose of establishing, maintaining, and perfecting the conditions necessary and appropriate for community life to perform its role in the complete development of man. This is what the law ought to do or ought to be. That the specific laws of individual societies or cultures do not always fulfill these objectives means only that the rules of law should be reformed and improved, not that the rule of law should be abandoned. Indeed, to abandon the law completely would be to invite chaos and societal suicide. Nonetheless, Melvin Lerner, a contemporary social psychologist who has specialized in empirical studies of the "justice motive" and may be considered a spokesman of one school of thought in this matter, holds that reliance on the law perpetuates a misleading if not a false concept of man's basic nature. Although most theorists maintain that experience with man's nature has amply demonstrated the need for law in society, Lerner's point cannot easily be dismissed.

Lerner says: "A contrasting hypothesis or model is that legal processes and institutions as we know them in western industrialized societies are dysfunctional and create social pathology."[3] He says later in the same article:

> Essentially, then, our laws are based upon and convey the image of man as a *selfish* animal but also a "rational" one capable of acting on the basis of enlightened self-interest. It appears that regardless of how valuable laws and legal institutions were, or are now, in maintaining social stability and protecting each citizen from exploitation by the more powerful elements in the society, their presence in our society requires that we live in a climate of distrust, fear, and alienation from one another. Their proliferation prevents us from discovering alternative ways of living and working with one another based upon trust and willing cooperation.[4]

Lerner is simply among the most recent in a long line of utopian legal theorists going back to Plato who regret that human beings cannot live in the real world without a rule of laws and rules of law. Granted that if human beings were much more perfect than they are and if philosophers were kings, there might be no need for legislators, judges, and policemen. If a major breakthough should occur in the human evolutionary process so that individuals and societies would come more manifestly to trust one another and cooperate with one another, the number of specific laws could be easily reduced. This new cooperative arrangement would simply become the *law* as contrasted with the *laws*. To say that the law or the laws thwart our chances of building more humane societies is to blame the law for the very thing that it, when it functions properly, best accomplishes. There may come a time when, for example, people will pay their fair share to taxes without being compelled by the law to do so, but hardly any one would think that time is now. For now, to attempt to build a just system of laws is the best that we can do; it would be extremely difficult to prove that such an attempt actually precludes the possibility of developing a society in which laws are no longer necessary.

Two further basic points of legal theory need to be clarified before the law and the laws can be seen as important avenues to culture learning. The first is the relationship between law and religion. The second is the relationship between law as legislation and law as judicial decision.

## Law and Religion

Like law itself, religion is a broad and general term. Historically, the interrelationships between religion in its various forms and law in its various forms are clear enough. Many of the early religious leaders were also the great lawgivers. Such persons as Hammurabi (who reigned from 1945–1902 B.C.), the Pharaohs of Egypt, and Moses were regarded as semidivine themselves or in close touch with God and therefore as possessing the power to make laws. The tendency for strong and important leaders to claim divine right and power is constant throughout history in both the East and the West. Thus, for example, the declaration, "the State—it is I" is attributed to Louis XIV of France. Shakespeare's *Richard II* dramatized the belief that treason against the King is also treason against God. Until the end of World War II, the Emperor of Japan was regarded by the Japanese as a kind of divinity. The reverence shown to Mao Tse-tung by the vast population of the People's Republic of China was enough to place him high above all mere mortals if not to make him one of the gods.

But it is in their function in human life that law and religion are most closely related. Both seek to define, formulate, and express the *oughts* and *ought nots* in human existence and in social transactions. Persons in every society engage in many kinds of activities which are governed merely by mores, customs, or conventions. The more important and more fundamental these activities become, however, the more likely they are to fall under the overarching mantles of both religion and law. The tendency in more recent centuries, at least in the West, has been, however, to regard religion as a matter of the internal forum—the private conscience and the inner spiritual life—and to regard the law as a matter of the public forum or overt activity. Richard Kroner enlarges on the distinction between the internal forum and the external forum in discussing religion and faith. He states:

> Religion can be regarded as a particular sphere in cultural life which is related to all other spheres but is also distinguishable from them, manifesting itself in particular institutions, habits and customs, norms and manners, dogma and doctrine, buildings and costumes and the like. Faith, though dependent upon religion, often deviates from its public manifestations. While organized religion is a public institution and has therefore a quasi-cultural appearance, faith is transcultural and private. Religion exists, like the state and the civil code, as a self-dependent, relatively separated entity; faith, on the contrary, exists only within the believer in his most secret and ineffable inwardness.[5]

In some religions or faiths, certain kinds of thoughts are regarded as evil or sinful, but the civil law does not and cannot enter into the realm of purely private thinking. Thus, for example, some may regard it as sinful or sacrilegious to wish someone else dead, but this mere wish cannot be a crime as long as it does not involve overt action of any kind. Religion and the law are related, further, in their best manifestations: They aim at the liberation, development, and fulfillment of man. Both religion and the law are too often seen as imposing restraints and restrictions on man's freedom. Both, in fact, when properly conceived, aim precisely at protecting and enhancing that freedom, that is, at creating the conditions that make freedom possible. Religion and law do impose compulsions—certain things must be done and others avoided—but these compulsions are never ends in themselves but rather means to the higher ends of the common good and the public welfare. Alfred North Whitehead makes a cogent statement in this connection: "Human society in the absence of any compulsion is trusting to the happy coordination of individual emotions, purposes, affections, and actions. Civilization can only exist amid a population which in the mass does exhibit this fortunate mutual adaptation."[6] He goes on to say, however, that "unfortunately a minority of adverse individual instances, when unchecked, are sufficient to upset the social structure. A few men in the whole cast of their character, and some men in some of their actions, are anti-social in respect to the peculiar type of any society possible in their time. There can be no evasion of the plain fact that compulsion is necessary and that compulsion is the restricting of liberty.''[7]

## Legislative and Court-Made Law

A second aspect of legal theory that needs to be more fully clarified before considering the law and the laws of a society as a mode of culture learning is the difference between legislation and court-made law. The problem here is a deep-rooted one because it has to do with who has the right to make laws that are binding on all the people and where that right comes from. The conventional wisdom that legislators—Parliament, Diet, Reichstag, Congress, or whatever—make the laws and that judges or jurors decide whether certain persons, real or moral, have or have not violated the laws is far too simple.

True, most modern constitutions, whether written or unwritten, rest the power of making laws with the legislature. But even this is a relatively recent development. Throughout most of human history, no distinction has been made between the power to make laws, interpret them, and enforce them. All these powers were combined in the person regarded as having ruling authority. He or she was, in effect, the legislative, the judicial, and the executive branches of government. The head of state made the laws, decided who was guilty of violating the laws, and enforced the laws as he or she saw fit. The idea of "separation of powers" and the idea that the people themselves, either directly or through their elected representatives, should make the laws under which they would live came very much later, particularly with the English philosopher, John Locke (1632–1704).

Legislatures, however, have never been able to write laws in such a way that they apply clearly and unequivocally to every instance that might arise. Disputes about what the law is and means are almost inevitable in all but the simplest cases. The individual citizen consequently does not always know with certainty whether a particular law does or does not apply to the action he is contemplating. If he refrains from a certain action, thinking it may be against the law when in reality it is not, he may be depriving himself of a perfectly legal benefit. If he goes ahead with the action, thinking it completely legal when in reality it is not lawful, he may have to suffer the dire consequences of having violated the law. Hence it comes about that a different type of legal institution, the court, is necessary to interpret the intent of the legislature and to decide whether and to what extent a particular law applies in a particular case.

The further conventional wisdom that the legislature makes the laws and the courts interpret and apply them becomes simply naive once it is clearly understood that the only real law is that law the courts do in fact uphold and enforce. The legislature may make what it considers to be the laws, but unless the courts agree and follow through, the laws are meaningless. Section 1 of Article I of the Constitution of the United States, for example, states: "All legislative Powers herein granted shall be vested in a Congress of the United States, which shall consist of a Senate and a House of Representatives." Yet Adolf A. Berle, the distinguished legal scholar, remarks that the broad and unrecognized fact is that "ultimate legislative power in the United States has come to rest in the Supreme Court of the United States."[8] Oliver Wendell Holmes, Jr., one of the pre-eminent figures in American jurisprudence and American intellectual history, writes that "the prophecies of what the courts will do in fact and nothing more pretentious are what I mean by the law."[9]

### The Law and Culture

Against this background, it is now possible to explore more fully how the law serves as a means of culture learning, or—put somewhat differently—how the study of a culture's law and its laws is one of the primary modes of culture learning. The essence of the matter is that the law does and must correspond to the basic values, attitudes, outlooks, and controlling ideas of the culture out of which it arises. The law is nothing other than a formulation, crystallization, and expression of these concepts and values, these controlling ideas, purposes, preferences, and desires. Good law changes as these concepts and values change.

This basic premise, however, is far from self-evident and demands further clarification. That some governments are much more interested in preserving their power than they are in the common good or general welfare is a fact of both history and present experience. The premise rests to a very large extent on the distinction previously made between the "rule of law" and the "rule of laws." It also presupposes the theory of the origin of law and of the power of lawmaking already outlined.

As we have seen, the "rule of law" implies a consensus within a culture or society on which behaviors are good and to be pursued, which behaviors are bad and to be avoided, and how conflicts are to be resolved. The rule of law implies lawful rule precisely because it represents the consensus within the culture on opinion and behavior, that is, the active, intelligent, and free consent of the governed. Thus the rule of law, the set of basic jural postulates, is the background out of which arise the specific rules of law. Culture learning through law is the process by which the learner comes to understand the jural postulates and their functioning in the culture.

The extent to which the rules of law correspond with and derive from the jural postulates (rule of law) will in actual practice vary from culture to culture. The culture learner would be greatly mistaken to think that every government that makes laws and rules by laws represents the consensus of those who live according to those laws. A rule of laws may be enforced by a dictator or military government that pays no attention to the rule of law. A government may be an unlawful government, not representing the will of the people and its consensus on opinion and behavior, and still have the power to impose its own rules of law on the people.

There are only two fundamentally different theories of the origin of law and how it comes about that some persons, whether kings, legislatures, or courts, are invested with the right to make laws binding on all persons in the society. Each of these two basic theories is manifest throughout history in a number of variations, but all are reducible to one or the other of these ultimate positions. The culture learner will find a consensus within the culture that tends toward either (1) the natural law theory or (2) the social realism theory.

The natural law theory in its essential form holds that man discovers in the physical and natural universe the laws which he is called on to obey. The laws are simply there—out there—and the great and wise lawgivers are those who articulate best what nature itself more or less directly decrees. Whatever is natural is lawful; whatever is unnatural or contrary to nature is unlawful. In both its Eastern and Western forms, natural law theory finds its basis in something external to man himself and to the group or society, that is, something in which man participates in some way but that man himself does not create. This something takes different forms in different cultures: Providence, the eternal law, the order and harmony of the universe, the One, God, transmigration, *élan vital,* and the like. According to this theory, even the most specific of statutory or positive laws are valid only to the extent they conform with, or at least do not contradict, the natural laws.

The social realism theory is much more human-centered than nature-centered. It holds simply that law originates in response to certain social needs and demands. Nature does not supply the laws according to which men's social and economic relationships might best be regulated; rather, human beings create these laws. Laws and legal systems, that is, constitutions, statutes, codes, legislatures, and courts, exist because men have found them necessary and helpful in achieving their social purposes. At whatever level of generality of application, laws derive from human reason and intelligence and from man's experience—in short, from what men think and what they desire. Those who hold to any of the various forms of the social realism theory of jurisprudence assume that every society exists for the purpose of the general welfare and that the general welfare demands equal justice for all members of the society. Nature itself has no way of telling us what is just and what is not.

What difference does it make in practice or in daily living whether the consensus in a culture sees law as originating in nature or in social needs, desires, and conditions? It makes a vast practical difference. Cultures that perceive the law as grounded in nature will tend to deduce their legal systems from what they consider to be the objective and more or less unchanging laws of nature. They will, in turn, validate or legitimate their individual legislative enactments and their judicial decisions by reference back to the objective criterion presumably found in nature. Are such things as usury, primogeniture, and prostitution, for example, natural or unnatural? If they are found to be—or thought to be—unnatural, then there will be laws against them. If they are thought to be natural, they will be permissible and even encouraged.

Cultures that perceive the law to be governed not in nature but in human needs and aspirations will be much more inductive and experimental in their legal systems. Laws will change as social conditions change, but, much more importantly, the laws will be used to bring about changes for the better in those social conditions. The laws and legal system are likely to be regarded more as a continuing redefinition of the original social contract which brought the laws into existence in the first place. John Rawls, after stating that the original social contract or the original social position is hypothetical, nonetheless finds such an hypothesis necessary to a workable theory of justice. After listing a number of conditions which would have to prevail to make the original social contract a fair and just one, Rawls summarizes in this way: " . . . these conditions define the principles of justice as those which rational persons concerned to advance their interests would consent to as equals when none are known to be advantaged or disadvantaged by social and natural contingencies."[10]

## Who Has the Right to Make Laws?

Every society or culture needs to arrive at some means early in its community existence for determining who has the right to make laws that will be binding on all its members. In the beginning of corporate or collective existence, lawmaking may simply be taken over by the most powerful, the wisest, the oldest and most experienced, or the most sacred and charismatic member or members of the group. If some one indicates what the law is going to be and if he has the physical or moral power necessary to enforce his decisions, he becomes the lawgiver. Later on, this power is legitimated or becomes legal and lawful through various rationalizations, not the least of which is that it works—namely, peace and order are maintained and the people are, at least relatively, happy.

Rule is also legitimated by appeal to such principles as a "Divine Right," an aristocracy of blood, a dynastic heritage, a record of accomplishment, or an implicit social contract.

Persons who first come to rule or govern as the result of a forceful seizing of the reins of government, however, need to protect themselves against the possibility of someone else's forcibly grasping the same reins of government from them. This can be done most readily either by repressing, dividing, and weakening all possible opposition or by convincing the people that the present government is truly in their best interests. The first has been the alternative chosen most often throughout history and well into modern times; the second, however, has been the more successful and long-lasting strategy. The concept that governments derive their power from the "consent of the governed" derives in part from philosophical theory regarding man's dignity and freedom, but it also derives in part from the fact that many of the great kings, emperors, conquerors, and founders of dynasties were able to consolidate those they governed solidly behind them. It was as if the people had in fact given their consent to being ruled in this particular way. These leaders, after first clearly establishing their power, set out next to bring the thinking and behaving of the people at large into conformity with what they wanted the people to think and feel. Perhaps the most notable contemporary example is that of China's Chairman Mao Tse-tung. Shortly after Mao's death, *Newsweek* wrote: "Virtually deified by his own countrymen and held in awe even by capitalistic societies of the West, he was the source and inspiration of one of history's most extraordinary personality cults . . . His plastic-covered 'little red book,' containing the 'thoughts' of Chairman Mao on how to make revolution and modernize China, was carried religiously by nearly every Chinese citizen and was translated into many languages."[11]

Even in societies or cultures in which the principle that governments derive their power to rule from the consent of the governed prevails, there remain the important cultural questions of how and when those who are governed manifest either their consent to, or their dissent from, the government's rules and policies. The election process, with the government's holding power either for a definite limited period of time or until such time as the people, through their ballots, show a loss of confidence, though not without its drawbacks, appears to be the best answer yet designed. Sir William Blackstone in his *Commen-*

*taries on the Laws of England* points out what he sees to be the evils of the election system as a means of either expressing consent or dissent. He writes:

> History and observation inform us, that elections of every kind are frequently brought about by influence, partiality and artifice, or at least such charge is proclaimed by a disappointed minority. All societies are liable to this evil. Both those of a private and domestic kind, as also the great community of the public. Time suppresses false suspicions in the former, and appeals to tribunals remedy them by legal means, if they be true, but in the great society of the nation, there is no superior tò resort to, but the law of nature, no mode of redress, but the actual exertion of force.[12]

## The Law as Source and Means of Culture Learning

We come now to the very practical question of how the law serves as a source or means of culture learning. Recalling our definition of a culture as a consensus on opinion and behavior, it will be immediately evident that in any given culture a basic consensus must exist among the people regarding who will have the power to make laws and what kinds of laws best enable the culture to pursue its goals and achieve its purposes. Coming to know these consensuses on the law is a vital and fruitful way of coming to know the deep structure of the culture itself. As Montesquieu pointed out early in *The Spirit of the Laws,* it is inevitable that the law and the laws would reflect and reveal the philosophical assumptions, values, attitudes and outlooks, ideals, and aspirations of the people of the culture. The law is much more than the culture's way of resolving conflicts; it is also the culture's way of achieving its social purposes and expressing its sense of justice and fairness. Underlying all considerations of the relationships between the law and the deep cognitive and affective structure of the culture is the premise that the law is a product of the culture's historical experience and its collective intelligence rather than simply an arbitrary and random product of individual lawmakers or judges.

There are three general ways that one who wants to learn a culture through a study of its laws and legal system might proceed. The first two ways would correspond roughly with the deductive and the inductive methods and also with what are called the *macro* and the *micro* approaches to any problem or to any discipline. The third way might be called the comparative method. The end result, namely, deeper insights into the basic consensuses in the culture, would be the same, but the ways of arriving at those insights would be quite different. In actual practice, both methods would be used; it would be impractical if not impossible to use either the deductive or inductive methods exclusively.

The first method, the deductive or macro-oriented method, starts with the legal system as a whole and attempts to trace or analyze particular laws and court decisions to their roots in the jural postulates and in the general public philosophy or world view. This is the method used, for example, by Blackstone in his monumental *Commentaries on the Laws of England*. At the beginning of each book—in the *Commentaries* each volume treats a different subject—Blackstone first lays down the general principles that he holds to be the basis or the foundation for particular laws. He goes on to attempt to show how the particular substantive and procedural laws are simply the logical and reasonable working out of the extensions or applications of these principles.

To take an example: At the beginning of Book the Fourth, which deals with "Public Wrongs," Blackstone states: "The discussion and admeasurement of this topic form the code of criminal law, of what is termed in England, the doctrine of the pleas of the crown, so called, because the king is supposed by law to be the person injured by every infraction of the public rights, and is therefore, in every case, the proper prosecution for every public offence."[13] The principle that every public offence is an injury to the person of the king is in the background thinking of all legislation and judicial decisions regarding criminal acts in the English culture. Blackstone does not explain why this principle holds true or how it came into being, but he lays it down as a principle of English jurisprudence that had held since time immemorial and which continued to dominate criminal law thinking in Blackstone's own day.

In the same introduction, Blackstone delineates the principle behind actions for the redressing of wrongs and the punishing of crimes: "Upon the whole, in taking cognizance of all wrongs, the law has a double view, *viz.:* not only to redress the party injured, by either restoring to him his rights, if possible, or by giving him an equivalent; but also to secure to the public the benefit of society, by preventing or punishing every breach of those laws, which the sovereign power has established."[14] Here again Blackstone regards this principle as simple common sense—or the result of many many years of cultural experience—but he leaves it as something to be taken for granted or assumed in English culture that this is the way "to secure to the public the benefit of society." And so it also becomes part of the thinking, viewing, and feeling out of which the criminal code develops.

The main point, however, is that anyone who studies Blackstone's *Commentaries* arrives at a much deeper and fuller understanding of English life and culture. The laws of England, like the laws of any other culture, reveal the basic agreements or consensuses among the people concerning what is right and wrong, good and bad, important and unimportant. The best evidence of this, of course, is that to this very day Blackstone's *Commentaries* are still widely read and studied by jurists, lawyers, students, historians, and literary men generally as a fundamental source of the understanding not only of English jurisprudence, but also of general English culture as well. To have studied Blackstone is to have taken a large step toward understanding how the English mind works.

Montesquieu in *The Spirit of the Laws* gives a more explicit statement of the deductive method, or the macro-oriented approach to the learning of a culture through the study of its laws, than Blackstone does. Early in his classic work, he explains the method he will be using throughout: "I shall first examine the relations which laws bear to the nature and principle of each government; and as this principle has a strong influence on laws, I shall make it my study to understand it thoroughly, and if I can but once establish it, the laws will soon appear to flow thence as from their source. I shall proceed afterwards to other and more particular relations."[15] *The Spirit of the Laws* is a historical examination of how the laws of a country or a culture are a direct function of its form of government, whether republican, monarchial, or despotic. Montesquieu maintains, however, that "Law is general human reason, inasmuch as it governs all the inhabitants of the earth: the political and civil laws of each nation ought to be only the particular cases in which human reason is applied. They should be adapted in such a manner to the people for whom they are framed that it would be a great chance if those of one nation suit another."[16]

The second method of culture learning through legal analysis is much more inductive and micro-oriented. Rather than starting from general principles, this method begins with specific pieces of legislation or specific court-made laws and attempts to trace them to their sources or principles and to find their meanings in the culture's deep structure. The culture learner, using this method, takes note in the beginning of the way a given law functions, or fails to function, in a given culture. The method is inductive and micro-oriented in that the culture learner at first views this law as isolated or independent from the rest of the legal system. His initial inquiry concerns what this law in itself commands or prohibits. He could start with a very simple law, as, for example, the law determining on which side of the street an automobile should be driven. Or he could start with a much more complex law, such as the law stipulating who should pay taxes, at what times, and in what amounts.

Starting with a specific law as given, the culture learner quickly observes that this particular law and those closely related to it form a set or subsystem of laws aimed at the achieving of some particular social good. For one simple example, the laws governing the side of the street on which automobiles should be driven, the speed laws, the on-street parking laws, and the laws requiring the observing of Stop and Go signals all aim at keeping automobile traffic flowing as efficiently and safely as possible. The need for an efficient and safe automobile traffic flow is derived in some societies from something more deeply valued, namely, promptness and punctuality. Traffic laws and regulations are not so important in those cultures in which being on time itself is not regarded as important. The culture learner, in this illustration, might next inquire into why the culture places so much emphasis on promptness and punctuality. Let us assume, to carry the example further, that, in the culture he is studying, promptness and punctuality are regarded as evidences of the deeper values not only of politeness but also of responsibility, methodicalness, and even of leadership. These values might be seen as part of a still deeper value relating to how the workload and the rewards for work should be distributed among the people of the culture. And finally, these values themselves might be quite easily traceable to cultural ethical systems and world views regarding what is and what is not of ultimate importance in the life of the individual and society.

This illustration is intended only as a broad outline of how the inductive or micro-oriented method of culture learning through the analysis of legal systems works. In short, it proceeds from the particular to the more general and abstract legal and cultural principles underlying the particular legislative enactment or judicial decision. This method is similar to that used by judges in what are called the "common law" countries. Under the common law, with its great emphasis on precedent, the judge, after examining the decisions laid down by the courts in cases similar to the one presently being heard, decides which rule of law should hold in this case. The judge does not start from any preconceived idea of what the law should be or even of what he would like it to be; rather, he starts either from what the precedents of this case are or from the wording of the legislation itself. The judge, in giving the reasons for his decision, sets forth the broader legal and cultural background and meaning into which this case fits.

An excellent example of how this method works in practice is Richard Kluger's book *Simple Justice*. Kluger takes the historic Supreme Court decision regarding the desegregation of schools in the 1954 case known as *Brown* v. *Board of Education* as his starting point. He uses this case not only as a landmark in black America's struggle for equality but also as a way of illuminating the deepest values in American culture. In some eight hundred carefully written and superbly documented pages, Kluger lays bare the tradition, thinking, passions and emotions, conflict of values, disparity between ideals and realities, and fears, hopes, and sacrifices that came together to bring about the desegregation of the schools in America. Kluger states that "probably no case ever to come before the nation's highest tribunal affected more directly the minds, hearts, and daily lives of so many Americans.[17] He goes on to call his book, a masterful piece of culture learning and teaching through law, "a chapter in the biography of a nation,"[18] and he states that a nation's worth is measured ultimately by how fairly it has dealt with all its citizens and how consistently it has denied the dignity of none.

The comparative method of culture learning through the study of analysis of the culture's law and legal systems starts from a quite different premise. The premise is that although cultures are different in many ways, there are great similarities among them for the very reason that all cultures are made up of human beings. Thus, for example, it is not surprising that the First Global Opinion Survey, which questioned 10,000 persons in nearly seventy countries, should have reported that "family life gives people all over the world the greatest satisfaction."[19] The same or very similar problems are likely to arise in every culture and all cultures. If family life gives people all over the world the greatest satisfaction, anything that interferes with family life—divorce, rape, kidnapping, child abuse, inheritance squabbles, and the like—will create the greatest dissatisfactions and conflicts the world over. True, different cultures would handle these and other matters in greatly different ways, some of them in fact not being considered matters for legal action at all in some cultures.

The comparative method takes as its starting point a particular human problem, difficulty, conflict, or right—or a particular social need or desire—and studies how these are resolved or ameliorated in two or more cultures. Laws that have developed in different cultures but out of similar religious, philosophical, and historical traditions or world views will normally be found to be remarkably similar, and those that have developed out of different traditions or different ways of doing and seeing things will be quite different. Thus, for example, James Kent in his *Commentaries on American Law* shows how American law and English common law are in all major respects similar. He writes:

> It was not to be doubted that the Constitution and laws of the United States were made in reference to the existence of the common law, whatever doubts might be entertained as to the question, whether the common law of England, in its broadest sense, including equity and admiralty as well as legal doctrines, was the common law of the United States. In many cases, the language of the Constitution and laws would be inexplicable without reference to the common law; and the existence of the common law is not only supposed by the Consti-

tution, but it is appealed to for the construction and interpretation of its powers.[20]

The comparative method of culture learning through law is similar to both the deductive and the inductive methods in that it is concerned not so much with what the particular law is but with why the law is as it is. What is the thinking behind the law, what values does it seek to preserve or enhance, what concepts of justice does it represent and enshrine? As the name implies, however, the comparative method aims at the learning of culture through law by way of contrast with other cultures. The primary objective is the learning of culture, but this objective is pursued by discovering the difference and the similarities between the legal structures or the legal systems in two or more cultures.

A relatively simple example may help to make the comparative method of culture learning through law somewhat more evident. The example concerns the law on how the nationality or citizenship of a person is determined. Every country has laws according to which persons either do or do not have the right to claim citizenship. These laws differ considerably from country to country in specific details, especially in the case of adults, but in general there are two basic ways in which the nationality or citizenship of a child is determined. The first is *jus soli*, which means simply a right arising from the territory or the land itself. The second is *jus sanguinis*, which is a right arising from a blood relationship. The first stipulates that a person born in a particular country or state, or in one of its territories, acquires the nationality of that country. The second holds that a person's nationality or citizenship is determined by the nationality of his parents, regardless of where he might happen to have been born. The laws of individual countries specify which principle will dominate and how strictly the principle will be adhered to. Interestingly, most countries in Europe and Asia follow the principle that one derives his citizenship from his parents, while the United Kingdom, the United States, and most countries in the Western Hemisphere follow the principle that citizenship derives from place of birth.[21]

There are many important and complex problems regarding

citizenship or nationality laws in the modern world. For example, in those countries that base the right to citizenship on blood relationship, is nationality transmitted to offspring only by the father, only by both mother and father, or only by the mother? In the growing number of cases in which the father and the mother are of different nationalities, does the child acquire citizenship in both nations, or does he have to make a choice between them? And what about the cases in which the father is unidentified or is stateless as a refugee? Culture learning is concerned with the thinking or the values behind the laws, however, rather than with the laws themselves—that is, why is the law as it is rather than something else? Countries or cultures are free to choose which principle—*jus soli, jus sanguinis,* or even conceivably some other—on which to base their citizenship laws. That choice and how and why it was made is highly significant to the culture learner.

Behind the laws of different countries for determining citizenship there appears to be a fairly general consensus on the thinking that every person should be a citizen of some country and that no person should be a citizen of more than one country. No person should have a double nationality. Since the sovereign state is the basic juridical unit in the modern international sphere, persons who are stateless enjoy neither the right nor the responsibilities of citizens. Persons with dual nationalities might often find themselves confronted with conflicting rights and responsibilities.

But why should it be, for example, that Japan should determine citizenship according to *jus sanguinis* and the United States according to *jus soli?* There must be something quite different in the cultural thinking and valuing of the two countries that would lead them to employ such widely different principles in deciding citizenship. The culture learner, using the comparative method as a means of culture learning through law, would proceed to examine various possibilities and hypotheses. For example, he might assume that there is something in the traditional structure of the Japanese family that puts a high value on blood relationships and that the Japanese regard the nation as simply a greatly extended family. If this is so, what is there in the Japanese world view that accounts for their valuing blood relationships so highly? One tentative answer might be that Japan, being a relatively small land mass, also places a high value on the land.

On the other hand, the culture learner might start with the assumption that, as a democratic nation, Americans have never accepted the idea of royalty or an aristocracy of blood. But if this is the explanation, why does England, which has a royal family, also base its citizenship laws on *jus soli?*

Using the comparative approach in culture learning through law the culture learnèr would, of course, pursue the comparison much more deeply and fully. The attempt to answer one question always opens up a number of other questions. Eventually, the culture learner will get down to—or back to—the key premises, assumptions, postulations, or constructs in the culture which are so central to the ways of thinking and living within that culture that they are simply taken for granted—that is, they can not be interpreted or explained by means of other more basic and more general cultural principles.

## The Law of Nations or International Law

The comparative approach to culture learning through law also easily lends itself to the further study of what is sometimes called the law of nations, international law, or even world rule of law. It is only a short step from comparing the law in individual cultures as a means of discovering their cultural roots and principles to considering what might be the bases or grounds for a viable international law or world rule of law.

Although the ability to participate in the development of a world rule of law is one of the principle objectives of culture learning, international law can be only briefly touched on here. The development of international law is still relatively in its infancy. Hugo Grotius, generally regarded as the father of international law theory, lived as recently as the seventeenth century. In the next century, Sir William Blackstone, the great commentator on the laws of England, wrote concerning the law of nations that:

> The human race is necessarily divided into many separate states and nations, entirely independent of each other, and yet liable to a mutual intercourse. Hence arises a third kind of law, in which, as no

superiority is acknowledged, the states will allow no dictation, but depend entirely upon the rules of natural law, or upon mutual Compacts, treaties, leagues and agreements between these several communities.[22]

And at about the same time, Montesquieu, the French philosopher and jurist, comments on the law of nations in this way:

> The law of nations is naturally founded on this principle, that different nations ought in time of peace to do one another all the good they can, and in time of war as little as possible, without prejudicing their real interests.
>
> The object of war is victory; that of victory is conquest; and that of conquest preservation. From this and the preceding principle all those rules are derived which constitute the law of nations.[23]

Very little advance has been made either in the theory or in the practice of international law since the time of Blackstone and Montesquieu. It is as true now as it was in Blackstone's day that the individual nation states acknowledge no superiority and allow no dictation. Some theorists felt that a major breakthrough in the direction of a world rule of law had been achieved when the Nuremburg trials following World War II enunciated the principle that the law would hold individuals as well as nations guilty of "crimes against humanity." Some interesting advances in thinking about a world rule of law have also been made, to mention only one of many, by the World Order Models Project.

But a widespread base of public support for a transnational or world rule of law has yet to come into being. Without such public support—that is, without a transnational consensus or community of thought and feeling that a true international law or a world rule of law is both necessary and desirable—there is likely to be little progress in that direction. Profoundly serious problems such as, for example, whether international law requires a worldwide constitution, political organization, and law enforcement agency are yet to be fully studied and answered. One of the first and most important steps, however, toward enlarging the base of public support on the basis of which a true transnational or world rule of law could develop lies in an extended and meaningful learning of other cultures.

NOTES

1. C. G. Weeramantry, *The Law in Crisis* (London: Capemoss, 1975), p. 131.

2. Palmer D. Edmunds, *Law and Civilization* (Washington, D.C.: Public Affairs Press, 1959), p. 10.

3. Melvin Lerner, "The Law As a Social Trap," in *Culture Learning Institute Report,* East-West Center 4-3, August,1976, p. 2.

4. Ibid., p. 7.

5. Richard Kroner, *Culture and Faith* (Chicago: University of Chicago Press, 1951), p. 209.

6. Alfred North Whitehead, *Adventures of Ideas* (New York: The Macmillan Company, 1956), p. 71.

7. Ibid., p. 71.

8. Adolf A. Berle, *The Three Faces of Power* (New York: Harcourt, Brace & World, 1967), p. 3.

9. Quoted by Fred V. Cavill Jr. in *Judicial Legislation* (New York: The Ronald Press Company, 1952), p. 36.

10. John Rawls, *A Theory of Justice* (Cambridge, Mass.: The Belknap Press of Harvard University Press, 1971), p. 19.

11. "The Last Titan," *Newsweek,* September 20,1976, p. 37.

12. Sir William Blackstone, *Commentaries on the Laws of England,* ed. William Hardcastle Browne (St. Paul: West Publishing Co., 1897), p. 61.

13. Ibid., p. 583.

14. Ibid., p. 586.

15. Baron de Montesquieu, *The Spirit of the Laws,* Great Books of the Western World, vol. 38 (Chicago: Encyclopedia Britannica, Inc., 1952), p. 3.

16. Ibid., p. 3.

17. Richard Kluger, *Simple Justice* (New York: Alfred A. Knopf, 1976), x.

18. Ibid.

19. Austin Scott, "The Gallup Poll Surveys the World," in the Honolulu *Sunday Star-Bulletin & Advertiser,* September 19, 1976, p. H–38.

20. James Kent, *Commentaries on American Law,* 12th ed., ed. O. W. Holmes, Jr. (Boston: Little, Brown and Company, 1873), p. 336.

21. Gyo Hani, "Japanese Nationality Question," in *Japan Times,* September 12, 1976, p. 12.

22. Blackstone, *Commentaries,* p. 9.

23. Montesquieu, *Spirit of the Laws,* p. 3.

# chapter 7

# Leisure and the Arts in Culture Learning

One of the more basic, as well as interesting and insightful, modes of culture learning is discovering the consensuses within a culture on what to do with leisure time or what to do during leisure time.

We use the term "leisure" here in a very broad sense to include whatever the people of a culture do when they have time they can use in any way they please. This sense differs somewhat from the more technical meaning given to it by Mortimer J. Adler in his well-known book on social philosophy, *The Time of Our Lives.* Adler states that the time of every human life is taken up in some combination of the five basic categories or types of activities: idling, sleeping, working, playing, and leisuring.[1] Adler's distinction among idling, playing, and leisuring, while technically valid, is too finely drawn to be relevant here. For our purposes, we can say that leisure is that time that people have when they are not *working* for a living and not *sleeping*. (Adler includes in the word "sleeping" not only slumbering but also all other predominantly biological functioning.)

The culture learner will find interesting things to learn from the consensuses within a culture regarding even the categories of working and sleeping. But the amount of choice within any culture about working and sleeping is greatly limited; consequently they are less culture specific. Many cultures will have some members of a leisure class who are so wealthy they do not have to work for a living and some members who are unable to work. But most people in most cultures are forced to work in order to live. Similarly, all people are forced to sleep, eat, bathe, dress, and the like. The consensuses on leisure, on the other hand, are an expression of the people's preferences, priorities, likes and dislikes, tastes, and attitudes when they have the opportunity to decide for themselves what they will do or not do. Leisure-time activity is particularly important as a basis of culture learning precisely because it is what the people choose to do, when they can make up their own minds, rather than what they are forced to do.

Josef Pieper has shown in his now-classic work, *Leisure the Basis of Culture,*[2] that culture and leisure are closely interrelated. Until such time in the development of any society that people have some free or leisure time to do what they want to do, that is, to express themselves in ways that they choose to express themselves, a distinctive human culture or a distinctive way of life cannot begin to develop. People who are forced to spend most of their waking hours at work in order to make a living for themselves and their families may have little time or energy for anything else. They are necessarily more preoccupied with how to make a living than with how to live. Pieper's contribution to the understanding of both leisure and culture is an important one precisely because he sees so clearly that not only must every society do everything possible to eliminate poverty so that everyone will be able to enjoy leisure, but also that every society must do everything possible to avoid thinking of man as primarily or exclusively a "worker." Work is a necessary part of every culture, according to Pieper, but it is neither the most important part of the culture nor that part that stamps it with its most distinctive or most admirable qualities.

The range of possibilities open to the people in a given culture for using what leisure time they have is limited by the outlooks and the circumstances of the general culture itself. Leisure-time pursuits that are very much a part of one culture may well be completely outside the experience, interests, and even imagination of people in another culture. Individuals in any culture have only the leisure-time opportunities and possibilities that their own culture offers. Richard Kroner explains it this way:

> The culture which man builds is experienced not as a system but as an actual reality which dominates his life and in which he participates by his conduct through actual contribution and creativity. Culture is a presupposition of human life as well as a product of it; it is both an outcome of human experience and part and parcel of that experience. Man experiences everything in the light of his culture, which stamps and molds his experience by generating the conceptions which inform him, when he perceives the world and himself or his fellowman.[3]

Culture is not experienced as a system by the one who is part of it but rather it is perceived as an actual reality that dominates his life—or even better *is* his life. Culture can, however, be studied as a system by the outside culture learner, who recognizes it as an actual reality. Consensuses on how to use leisure time are a fundamental and integrating part of every cultural system.

In discussions of leisure, the arts, and culture learning the distinction is frequently made between "high culture" and "popular culture." This will also be a useful distinction to the culture learner.

There is in every culture, for example, a vast difference between the religion of the theologians and the simple faith of the ordinary believer. There is a vast difference, as well, between the legal theories of the lawyers and jurists and the day-to-day legal knowledge and understanding of the man on the street. There is also a vast difference between designing and engineering an Olympic stadium and building a neighborhood playground.

The implication sometimes associated with the distinction between high culture and popular culture, however, is that high culture is of and for the elite and popular culture is of and for the masses. A further implication is that popular culture is more basic, vital, and meaningful because it appeals to, and captures the interest of, much greater numbers of people. Consequently, it is argued, the real heart and spirit of a people is in its popular culture rather than in its high culture. By this reasoning, the culture learner who wants to learn another culture through discovering its consensuses on leisure-time activities is better advised to concentrate on its popular rather than high culture.[4]

To the extent that it leads people to associate the elite with high culture and the masses with popular culture, such a distinction tends to confuse rather than clarify. The consensus within a culture is not to be found in what the few, who are highly favored and privileged by birth, wealth, and education, do with their leisure time. Neither, however, is it to be found in some statistical way by counting the number of people who do or do not do certain kinds of things in their leisure time. The consensus is rather to be found in what all or most of the people recognize as the quality or worthwhileness of whatever is or is not done. The intellectual, spiritual, artistic, and scientific leaders in a culture are not so much out of touch with what the rest of the people think and feel as they are in advance of what the others will soon be thinking and feeling. In short, the culture learner is concerned with knowing what is truly *popular* in that it represents what the people, taken together and as a whole, think and value. It is as much a mistake to assume that, if everyone does something or likes something, it cannot be much good as it is to assume that, if only a few do it, it has to be good.

One difficulty with the distinction between high and popular culture lies in the fact that it is not a complete disjunction. The opposite of *high* is *low*, not *popular*. The distinction leads to further difficulty in that it tends to suggest that high, lofty, noble, and serious themes and efforts are of no interest to the common people and that light and playful themes and efforts are of no interest to the so-called elite. If the straightforward word "low" were used instead of "popular" and if "low" were understood to mean that which no one takes too seriously, the distinction would serve a larger purpose. High culture would refer to the people's best efforts in serious matters. Low culture would refer to the people's best efforts in those matters that should be enjoyed for what they are but taken lightly. The distinction would then be virtually the same as that made by Adler between "leisuring," doing things that lead to human personal fulfillment, and "playing," doing things that have no end or goal beyond themselves. Something is popular—whether it is a song, a dance, a novel, or a picnic—precisely because it is perceived as good, that is, genuinely interesting, entertaining, enjoyable, amusing, and relaxing.

Another problem with the distinction between high culture and popular culture, however, is that such labels tend to reify the present, thus dismissing historical development. Much that is now regarded as high culture, both in leisure activities and in the arts, was originally popularly accepted, appreciated, and enjoyed. For example, Shakespeare wrote his plays for the general public. Dante wrote his *Divine Comedy* in the vernacular rather than in Latin so it could be understood by everyone. Some of Beethoven's greatest symphonies used simple folk melodies as their motifs. Many of the greatest paintings and statues are of everyday scenes and people. The great cathedrals were intended primarily as places for all people to worship. Some of the arias of the great operas were once as popular as the latest top hit pop tunes. High culture is not high because it can be enjoyed and appreciated by only the few but precisely because its quality has been recognized and enjoyed by the many from generation to generation.

Conversely, something that is now thought of as belonging in the domain of popular culture, detective stories for example, will become part of the high culture if it comes to be taken seriously rather than lightly. It must be good or it will soon disappear. What is popular survives precisely because it is authentic and open to the appreciation, enjoyment, and criticism of all.

## Leisure and the Arts

The article on "Culture" in a recent edition of the *World Book Encyclopedia* contains the following statement: "People tend to spend more time, energy, and skill on art than on any other activity. This is because communication holds people together who share a culture, and the arts are the most efficient means of communication.[5] These sentences are rather startling, to say the least; that people spend more time, energy, and skill on art than they do on working for a living is highly doubtful. There is no doubt, however, that the arts play a major part in the life of every culture and that they are a warm, appealing, and effective, if not necessarily always the most efficient, means of communication.

It would seem much more accurate to say that, apart from the time spent on making a living, people spend more energy and skill on the arts than on any other activity. One of the main sources of human enjoyment and satisfaction in any culture is in the making or creating of things. And the general term for the making or creating of things is *art*. The people of a culture express their deep-structure cultural values and cognitive patterns through their arts—that is, through the things they make or create in their leisure time, the main opportunity they have to be creative.

There are, of course, many different kinds of art, ranging all the way from making a chair or basket weaving to designing and building a Taj Mahal. For broad purposes of classification, however, the arts are usually divided into the practical arts and the fine arts. The practical arts are those in which the thing made or created serves some useful purpose. The practical art of watchmaking, for example, serves the same useful purpose as did the ancient sun dial, namely, the accurate telling of time. The fine arts are those in which the things made or created serve no specific, immediately useful purpose. Michelangelo's *Pietà* or his *David*, for example, are simply works of art, creations of splendid beauty, complete unto themselves. Some might argue, rather gratuitously, that the *Pietà* also serves the purpose of filling the beholder with feelings of tenderness and compassion, and the *David* is a constant reminder of the triumph of intelligence over brute force.

The fact is that the distinction between the practical arts and the fine arts, like the distinction between popular culture and high culture, is not completely mutually disjunctive. Some of the practical arts—the art of pottery making, for example—reach such artistic heights that the beauty of the vase or bowl is as enjoyable as the product is useful. Some of the fine arts—drama, for example—may have a practical educational impact more telling and poignant than any classroom lecture. To the extent, however, that they are authentic works of art, whether practical or fine, every work of art expresses the conceptions, values, and artistry of the artist and his times.

Another distinction among the arts especially important for purposes of culture learning is that between the *operative* and the *cooperative* arts. In the operative arts, the artist himself imposes a new form on the thing he makes or creates. Thus, the watchmaker makes a watch out of the elements he finds given in nature and the sculptor carves a statue out of granite. In the cooperative arts, the most notable of which are the arts of teaching, medicine, and agriculture, the artist simply cooperates with nature in producing the desired results. Thus, for example, the art of teaching consists not in the teacher's transferring knowledge from his own mind to that of the student but in creating the conditions under which the student can teach himself, that is, make his own discoveries. The student is the primary agent in the learning process and the teacher is a cooperative artist. It cannot be stressed too much that culture learning-teaching is a cooperative act rather than an operative one.

A final distinction that needs to be mentioned here is the familiar one between art itself, in its great variety of forms, and art appreciation. The two are clearly distinct: The one has to do with making or creating, the other has to do with what has already been made or created. Culture learners seek primarily to understand and appreciate the arts of another culture, but they may find that the easiest way and surest way to do this is to engage themselves in the arts of that culture.

Neither the practical nor the fine arts will flourish where they are not respected, valued, and appreciated throughout the culture. The artist, whether carpenter or dancer, is very much a product of the cultural milieu; if the society or culture does not look for beauty and rejoice in it, the potential artist's talents may never come to light. Even the practical and functional arts will be drab and uninspired if the culture does not insist that they be beautiful as well as practical.

The historical periods in which the fine arts have flourished have all been periods in which the artists, minor as well as great, were well received, encouraged, honored, and challenged to even greater achievements. And, on the contrary, when cultures feel no need for things of beauty, when potential artists are spurned or ignored, when leisure becomes a way simply for passing the time, that is, a time of games, spectacles, amusements, and idleness, then the arts either never get started or, once having got a start, rapidly rigidify into set patterns and forms and eventually decline. Edward Gibbon gives us one example from the many that could be cited in both the Orient and the Occident. "If a man were called to fix the period in the history of the world during which the condition of the human race was most happy and prosperous, he would, without hesitation, name that which elapsed from the death of Domitian to the accession of Commodus [180–192 A.D.]."[6] Gibbon adds: "It is not alone by the rapidity or extent of conquest that we should estimate the greatness of Rome. . . . But the firm edifices of Roman power were raised and preserved by the wisdom of ages. The obedient provinces . . . were united by laws and adorned by arts."[7]

## The Arts and Cultural Values

Culture learners approach the arts of the particular culture they are studying from an altogether different perspective than do either the artists or the general populace of the culture itself. The artists of a culture create what is an artistic aesthetic experience and the people appreciate it in their own distinctive way. Although all great art expresses something universal, it originates in, and is part of, a specific culture. The artist communicates feelings and emotions, as well as ideas, and although his message may be quickly and intuitively grasped by those who share his cultural background, it can easily be lost on those who do not. D. W. Gottshalk has pointed out that aesthetic experience " . . . is simply intrinsic perception, or attention to an object or a field pre-eminently for the apprehension of the full intrinsic perceptual being and value of the object or field."[8] He explains further: "In the aesthetic experience the great concern is to let all that is present in the object appear to the self in the fullest and most vivid manner. The object consequently becomes the guide, and the self submits to its lead. . . . Transformation by the object, not transformation of the object is the chief thing."[9] Later he writes: "Yet it is true that, without imagination and feeling, aesthetic experience at least would be reduced to an apprehension of only the barest actualities."[10]

The culture learner comes to the arts of the particular culture not primarily for the sake of an aesthetic experience but for the purpose of discovering what the culture's art reveals about the culture itself. If this effort also involves a direct aesthetic experience, so much the better. In fact, since artistic expression is essentially a social expression—that is, an expression of the thinking, feeling, valuing, admiring, believing, and worshipping of a people or culture—it is highly doubtful that an outsider to the culture can ever have exactly the same kind of aesthetic experiences that the members of that culture have. Although in their most creative moments artists must work alone and are frequently lonely people, their times, their culture, their milieu, speak through them. It is this message, rather than the aesthetic experience of the arts themselves, that is sought by the culture learner. Yet the more the culture learner comes to know, understand, and empathize with the people of a culture, the closer he will come to appreciating and aesthetically experiencing its various art forms.

How is it, then, that the arts and the artists of a culture open that culture to one of the best possibilities for culture learning? It has been indicated earlier that the people of a culture turn freely and spontaneously to the arts when they no longer need to be totally concerned with survival and have the time and energy to do things they enjoy doing. What is expressed in the arts is what they most value, appreciate, and enjoy.

It will be found, first of all, that the values of a culture are expressed in the more or less recurrent themes that run through its various works of art. It will also be found that a culture's value system, its system of priorities, is expressed, in a real but less direct way, in the forms of the arts that are practiced and most widely appreciated. A further word about both the themes of the arts and the forms of the arts is in order.

The subject of the arts—what they are about or what they are concerned with or what they depict—might possibly include almost anything known to the artist—cravings, needs, interests, goals, aims, drives, desires, sufferings, impulses, strivings, hopes, fears, joys, loves, and hatreds. Artists, whether poets, painters, sculptors, novelists, and dancers or whether those in the more practical arts, however, tend to respond to the moods, movements, stirrings, and demands at work in their cultures and in their times. The artists may, it is true, be in rebellion against the dominant values of the culture of which they are a part and they may also be among the first to catch a glimpse of the new directions the culture may be taking. But in every age and in every culture the artists will have selected out of all possible themes the ones they think deserve stressing and the ones about which they feel they have something to communicate. Gottshalk makes this same point when he quotes Randall Jarrell to the following effect: "Perhaps one reason that the painting and sculpturing of the twentieth century have been restless and bizarre is that modern society offers no compelling themes to stabilize the artist's mind and elicit his best work."[11]

The individual artist may or may not be consciously aware of the fact that his artistic work can be studied as a way of gaining further understanding of the values prevalent in his culture. He is much more likely in fact to agree with Sir Julian Huxley that the "essential function of the arts is one of bearing witness to the wonder and variety of the world and of human experience . . . it is to create vehicles for the effective expression and communication of emotionally charged experiences, which are of value in the process of human fulfillment."[12] If he is in the fine arts, he may truly regard his art as "art for art's sake"; if he is in the practical arts, he may simply want to make the most efficient and practical product that will serve the purposes he has in mind.

Nonetheless, the values held in the culture will almost inevitably be reflected in the subjects or themes chosen by that culture's artists. If, for example, it is a culture in which religious values are highly respected, the themes, the subject matter, the content of much of that culture's art will be religious in nature. Thus, much of the art in strongly Buddhist cultures is inspired by the life and teachings of Buddha and in Christian countries by the life and teachings of Christ. If, on the other hand, the culture is one in which man himself is of central concern, then the face, figure, and activities of man will be prominent artistic themes in portraits and statues as well as in poems, biographies, and novels. If the culture is one in which nature is treasured or revered, then nature in its many forms will be the subject of much of the art and a primary preoccupation of the artists. Thus, for example, classical Chinese art places great emphasis on mountains, waterfalls, and misty clouds, and the human beings shown in the foreground are usually so relatively small as to be almost inconspicuous. The Chinese had a deep feeling that man, being only a minor part of nature, should be humble in the face of it.

A secular, technological culture will also have its dominating artistic themes, as will a culture or society in process of transition or one seeking to reestablish or preserve its identity. There is even a sense in which so-called "abstract art," which from the viewpoint of the artist himself might seem deliberately themeless, carries a theme both for the members of the artist's culture and for the culture learner. Jacques Maritain holds, however, that the notion of "abstract art," if carried to its logical extremes, would result in an art completely isolated from everything except its own peculiar rules of operation and the demands of the object to be created as such—in other words, separate and apart from, and perfectly disinterested in regard to man.[13] Maritain goes on to say that such art ". . . will in the end decay if it rejects either the constraints and limitations required from without by the good of man or the service of our common culture, which requires it to make itself intelligible, accessible, open, to shoulder the burden of the inheritance of reason and wisdom by which we live."[14]

Another and perhaps simpler way of getting at how the values of a culture are reflected in the themes or subjects chosen by artists for their works, whatever form they may take, is to ask the question: What is the artist himself trying to do? We can assume that (at least in those cultures in which the artist is free to pursue his art as he thinks best, rather than having the directions of his art determined for him by some outside patron or some particular ideology), the artist is not trying to teach. He is not trying to teach even those who belong to the same culture as he, to say nothing of teaching potential culture learners.

The artist is simply trying to make something—that something may be a poem, a concerto, a dance, a painting, or a suit of clothes. Whatever it may be, it is something that the artist regards as important to make. But it is not something, except in the rarest of instances, that he is making simply for his own personal delight. He wants whatever he makes to be seen, enjoyed, and remembered by others. If his art is good and if what he is making is regarded as important or worthwhile by his fellow man, it will in fact elicit a broad base of public support and approval. The point is that he is not trying to say what is or is not important in the culture; rather he is trying to *show* what is important. The culture learner, having been shown in and through the culture's art what the artists regard as important and having observed the public's acceptance of the works of art, reaches his own insights, impressions, and intuitions regarding the culture's consensus on what is of value and importance. One very simple example can be drawn from the field of architecture. The architectural design of homes in a culture gives the culture learner a good idea of the value placed on family life in the culture. Similarly, the design of the supermarket gives the culture learner a good idea of the value placed on efficiency and functionality— as contrasted with sociability—in the culture.

The arts of a culture also offer the culture learner a second way of coming to a better understanding of the value structure in the culture. This, in contrast with the thematic approach, is a study of the different forms the arts themselves take. While it is probably correct to say that the forms of the arts are potentially universal—that is, that every culture knows and includes music, painting, sculpture, poetry, dance, pantomime, architecture, and all of the other generic forms—it is also true that different cultures emphasize certain forms more than others and that every culture gives something of its own style to whatever art forms are most widely practical and appreciated. Underlying all the forms and styles of the arts, however, is the symbolic and representational meaning of the various arts as they express theological, historical, ethical, psychological, social, and political themes in a visible way or an aural way.

Thomas Munro, in his massive *Evolution of the Arts,* makes it clear that art forms and styles in different cultures have not followed a simple pattern of movement from the simple to the more complex. He states that:

> History does not show a steady, continuous unilinear increase in the complexity of particular works of art. It shows an over-all tendency to complication in that civilized art has produced works far more complex than any produced in prehistoric cultures . . . but history also shows that many very complex works were produced in antiquity,

such as the *Odyssey* with its intricately woven design of episodes and characters. On the other hand, some very simple forms are produced today: in abstract painting for example.[15]

Whether an art form or style is simple or complex—whether in fact the art work itself is considered to be good, bad, or indifferent—the very form of the work of art visibly or aurally reflects in part the culture's value system. There are, for example, many forms of poetry and many kinds of poets in virtually every culture. The poetry of some cultures tends to be highly rigid, carefully formulated, precisely confined to certain set patterns of rhyme, meter, and versification. The poetry of other countries and cultures tends to be much freer, loosely constructed, experimental, and at least superficially much less disciplined. The very form that the poetry takes may be indicative of the culture's values regarding organization and systematization in the culture; it may speak—far beyond the poetry itself—of the cultural consensus about openness to change and about its adherence to fixed traditional patterns and rules. The form of the poetry may go still further, giving some profound clues about the value placed on explicitness and directness in interpersonal relationships.

One very good example of how some of a culture's values are reflected in its art forms or styles is the art of calligraphy in Japan. Every literate culture has developed to some extent the art of calligraphy or, as it is sometimes called, handwriting or penmanship. The basic purpose of calligraphy is simply clarity and legibility of the written character or word. In Japan, however, calligraphy has become much more than a useful skill; it is a high form of art as well. But how does the study of Japanese calligraphy help the student of Japanese culture understand better the deeper Japanese cultural consensus on what is valuable and worth preserving?

First of all, calligraphy is almost the essence of simplicity; this does not mean at all that it is easy. Rather, it means that this art form has splendid clarity, immediacy, and matter-of-factness or realism about it. The Japanese tend to place a high value on simple and natural things, not only in decorating their homes and gardens but also in their uncluttered and realistic world view itself. A Japanese scroll containing a simple character, calligraphed by a master calligrapher, may well be a family's most important treasure. Second, the rules of calligraphy are definite and well established; this is a reflection of the high value the Japanese place on tradition and clear, fixed relationships. Each calligrapher develops his own techniques and style, but there are no wide deviations, shocks, or surprises in the calligraphed work of art. There is a set order of strokes of the pen and there is a general expectation of understatement rather than overstatement in the judging of the finished work of art. Finally, the art of calligraphy demands of the artist an extraordinary honesty, authenticity, and concentration that are a reflection of the value the Japanese place on the striving for tranquility and at-oneness with the world.

## The Arts and Concern for Beauty

Just as the arts practiced and appreciated in a culture help the culture learner arrive at a deeper understanding of that culture's value system—through both the content and the form of the arts—so, too, the study of a culture's arts leads to a deeper understanding of its consensuses on the beautiful. These consensuses are of at least two kinds: (1) whether the culture is in general concerned with the cultivation of beauty, that is, whether the pursuit of the beautiful is itself regarded as a value and is taken seriously; and (2) whether there is a consensus on what is and is not considered beautiful.

It is at least conceivable that the people of a given culture would live in a setting of such natural beauty that they would pay little or no attention to the beauty of the things they themselves made. They would have no need for beauty other than that provided by nature. It is also conceivable that the people of a culture might, on the other hand, live in a natural setting so devoid of beauty, so ugly and squalid, that their sense of beauty might never be awakened. Though conceivable, these possibilities do not at all conform to actual experience. There is no record of any culture in which the beauties of nature were so overwhelming and complete that man has not also sought beauty through art. And there is no record of any culture from which art and beauty have been completely excluded because the people had become completely habituated to ugliness. Man everywhere enjoys and delights in the beauties of both nature and art, but the degree to which the beauty of art is a major concern to the people will vary from culture to culture. As Iredell Jenkins states, "Art has universal relevance because men who participate in a common nature share a world in which various things themselves have much in common."[16] Jenkins's thesis is that art and aesthetic activity (the search for beauty) are a natural and spontaneous phase of man's ordinary response to the environment, that art and beauty are not casual and adventitious happenings in human development, that art exists for life's sake, and that life could not exist without art.

There can be no doubt, however, that some cultures put a much higher value on beauty and the making of things beautiful, as a matter of public policy, concern, and practice, than other cultures. This is not at all the same thing as saying that people in different cultures find beauty in different things and in different ways. It is saying that beauty does not interest or enter into the awareness of people in some cultures as much as it does in others. There may be in whole cultures a consensus on the fact that questions of beauty are matters of relative indifference; the questions of whether things should be beautiful may seldom come up at all. The attention and energies of such cultures are simply directed to the making and doing of things without any special reference to whether what is made is beautiful or not.

The interesting thing to note in searching out whether a given culture places a high value on beauty is that there seems to be no direct correspondence between so-called stages of technological development and concern for beauty. In fact, some of the most highly developed countries or cultures in the world are among those that put the least emphasis on beauty; their chief concern is with function and utility. On the other hand, some of the so-called primitive or underdeveloped cultures show an exceptionally high regard for the beauty of what they make, even though their art forms are themselves sometimes considered simple and elementary. A highly industrialized society, in which the principles of the division of labor and specialization have become dominant, may quite easily come to feel that in everyday life form indeed does follow function and that beauty is not a general but a specialized concern—of professional artists and institutions such as museums and art galleries.

The culture learner is likely to find important insights into the culture he is studying not only by considering whether the culture as a whole places importance and value on beauty in human existence but also by considering the culture's consensus on *what* is beautiful. In his late nineteenth-century work on the philosophy of the beautiful, the English philosopher William Knight set out to prove that standards of beauty are more universal than is commonly thought. He wrote:

> It has been repeatedly affirmed that, although the Hottentot Venus is superlatively ugly to the European eye, the distinction between her and what is known as the Venus of Melos or the Castellani Aphrodite is only one of degree, containing nothing intrinsic. . . . It is notorious that the verdicts passed by the human race as to Beauty are as various as the nations, and almost as the families of mankind. But such statistics are irrelevant. They cannot disprove the fact . . . that given an adequate education in Beauty, these scattered judgments and verdicts will approach toward a common standard; and that the crude taste of the savage will yield, in a perfectly normal way, to the insight of the civilized.[17]

Knight's view, now considered quaint and even arrogant by most philosophers, is quoted as a clear statement of the historical position that *what* is considered beautiful approaches a common standard. It might be true that if everyone received the same kind of education, or if everyone by implication lived in the same culture, everyone would have the same standards for distinguishing between what is beautiful and what is not. But the supposition is simply contrary to fact. People live in different cultures and are consequently heirs to different kinds of aesthetic education.

The much more common view taken by Thomas Munro is that what is considered artistic and beautiful in any culture reflects the distinctive thoughts, feelings, and desires of that culture.[18] Munro uses as examples the beauty of the African Negro drumbeats and sculpture, the Lascaux Paleolithic cave paintings, and the highly complex Balinese music.[19] There is in fact no approach to a common standard of beauty among all cultures and there is, furthermore, no need for a common standard. From the viewpoint of culture learning, the effort is to determine what the people regard as beautiful and how it happens that beauty is understood and appreciated in the many diverse ways it is.

That different cultures will have different interpretations of what is beautiful and what is not—and different standards or criteria by which beauty is judged—flows also from the very nature or concept of beauty. There is, to be sure, no universal transcultural agreement even on the nature of beauty, but perhaps the simplest and best recognized definition is that given by the great theologian-philosopher of the thirteenth century, St. Thomas Aquinas. Maritain quotes Aquinas's definition that beauty is that "which when seen pleases." Anything is thus beautiful if seeing it gives pleasure, joy, delight to the one who sees it. Conversely, something is ugly if the seeing of it excites feelings of aversion, rejection, or repulsion in the one who sees it. The term "seeing" here is taken in the broad sense to include not only the specific act of looking or seeing but also the intellectual act of comprehending, that is, seeing in the sense of understanding. A culture learner listening to the music, for example, of the culture he is studying might not find it at first beautiful at all since he is not yet able to perceive the integrity, proportion, and clarity which distinguishes music from cacophony.

Maritain, following Aquinas, goes on to explain that since whatever is beautiful is essentially delightful because it pleases when seen, the beautiful is also a kind of good rather than a kind of truth. When seen, the truth simply illumines the mind, but the beautiful attracts, pleases, and stirs desire and love in the same way that something seen as good does. The seeing and appreciation of beauty is not merely, however, a matter of intuition, emotion, and ineffability. The mind is also very much involved. As Maritain puts it:

> Every sensible beauty, no doubt, implies a certain delight of the eye or the ear or the imagination: but there can be no beauty unless mind also is in some way rejoiced. A beautiful color "washes the eye" as a powerful scent dilates the nostrils: but of these two "forms" or qualities, only color is called "beautiful" because being received, as opposed to the perfume, in a sense capable of disinterested know-

ledge, it can be, even through its purely sensible brilliance, an object
of joy to the mind. Again, the more highly developed a man's culture
becomes, the more spiritual grows the brilliance of the form that rav-
ishes him.[20]

If this analysis of the nature and concept of beauty is correct,
it follows that people with different cultural backgrounds, traditions, and experiences will hold different things to be beautiful.
They will not "see" the same things or, if the same things, they
will not "see" them in the same way. Beauty is, let us stress
again, in the eyes of the beholder, and the concept of culture
means essentially that different beholders see things differently
as a result of the ways in which reality is mediated through their
individual cultures.

The task of the culture learner is to seek to discover what the
consensus is in the culture regarding beauty and standards of
beauty. Some cultures, for example, will consider beauty to
reside in ornamentation, and the more intricate and complex the
ornamentation, the better. Others will hold that only simple and
unadorned things can be genuinely beautiful and that all ornamentation for its own sake detracts from the quality of beauty.
Some cultures will appear to think that beauty consists more in
the unexpected and the novel rather than in an enduring quality.
Thus, for example, people of a culture who live near the ocean
and see it all the time may not consider it beautiful at all, while
those who see the ocean only infrequently may find great aesthetic satisfaction from it each time they see it. People in some
cultures may agree, on the other hand, that beauty is to be found
everywhere and that the older and more familiar things are more
beautiful. Similarly, there may be consensuses in some cultures
that movement and rhythm are the source of the greatest beauty,
while others agree that static forms, whether in nature or in art,
give rise to deeper aesthetic enjoyment. Some cultures will find
the human body among the things of beauty and others will regard it as base and unworthy of attention in painting, sculpture,
or even photography.

Both the attention that a culture pays to beauty and the ways
in which it measures beauty are direct and virtually spontaneous
expressions of the spirit, that is, the thinking and feeling, of that

culture. This is particularly true of that part of the beautiful which is of man's own making, his artistic creations, rather than that part which is given in nature. Whether the people of a culture see something beautiful in such natural things as a rose, a tree, a sunset, or a snowstorm tells culture learners something of importance about the psyche and the sensibility of that culture. But they are likely to be more richly rewarded in their search for a greater knowledge and understanding of the culture they are studying if they can discover why the people of the culture regard some of the creations of their own artists as beautiful and others as not.

It has often been said that art expresses its age—that is, its culture, its civilization. Equally correct, since the relationship between the two is mutual and reciprocal, is the statement that each age or culture expresses its art. Whether in fact the general culture determines the arts or the arts determine the general culture is a question that can never be answered, because the two are in constant interaction. Munro states the dynamics of this interaction between the culture at large and the arts in this powerful and precise way:

> The usual view is that art puts into explicit, objective, communicative form certain distinctive thoughts, feelings, and desires which have been current for a while but not clearly stated. They may have been vaguely hinted or implied by people's actions, or abstractly and partially stated by philosophers and scientists; but works of art can put them into concrete, personal symbols which make people more vividly aware of their human significance. Through their influence, the group can become fully aware of what it is trying to achieve and why; of where it has been moving for a long time without realizing the fact.[21]

We have considered in this chapter how it is that the arts of any culture are one of the most engrossing and most illuminating forms of culture learning. Culture learners seek to discover how the people of the culture use their free time, that is, their opportunity to be creative, artistic, and imaginative; they seek to discover, as well, what emphasis the culture puts on beauty and what it considers beautiful. The artists of a culture are not commenting on their culture. They are doing something in many ways more direct, real, powerful, and immediate. They are *showing* that culture, its consensuses on values, ideas, and feelings. A culture becomes coherent and comprehensible precisely because of the form its artists give it. As Susanne K. Langer wrote, "Above all, however, art penetrates deep into personal life because in giving form to the world it articulates human nature: sensibility, energy, passion, and mortality. More than anything else in experience, the arts mould our actual life of feeling."[22]

## NOTES

1. Mortimer J. Adler, *The Time of Our Lives* (New York: Holt, Rinehart, and Winston, 1970), p. 39.

2. Joseph Pieper, *Leisure the Basis of Culture* (New York: Pantheon Books, 1951). See especially Pieper's definition and explanation of his concept of leisure in chapter 3, pp. 24–32. He states: "And therefore leisure does not exist for the sake of work—however much strength it may give a man to work; the point of leisure is not to be a restorative, a pick-me-up, whether mental or physical; and though it gives new strength, mentally and physically, and spiritually, too, that is not the point" (pp. 30–31).

3. Richard Kroner, *Culture and Faith* (Chicago: University of Chicago Press, 1951), p. 71.

4. No one, perhaps, has done more to highlight the distinction between high culture and popular culture than Gilbert Seldes. His *The Seven Lively Arts,* first published in 1924 and republished in 1957, is well worth reading, if for no other reason than for its comparison of a good musical revue and a production of grand opera at the Metropolitan Opera House—to the great disparagement of the latter (p. 133). Seldes, it should be noted, makes no distinction between the elite and the masses. The main thesis of his book is summarized in his statement that: "We know also that while the part of humanity which is fully civilized will always care for high seriousness, it will be quick to appreciate the high levity of the minor arts. There is no conflict, the battle is only against solemnity which is not high, against ill-rendered profundity, against the shoddy and the dull." Gilbert Seldes, *The Seven Lively Arts* (New York: Sagamore Press, 1957), p. 294.

5. Carleton S. Coon, "Culture," in *the World Book Encyclopedia,* vol. 4 (Chicago: Field Enterprises Educational Corporation, 1971), p. 945.

6. Edward Gibbon, *The Decline and Fall of the Roman Empire,* abr., ed. D. M. Low (London: Chatto and Windus, 1960), p. 1.

7. Ibid., p. 11.

8. D. W. Gottshalk, *Art and the Social Order* (Chicago: University of Chicago Press, 1947), p. 3.

9. Ibid., p. 15.

10. Ibid., p. 20.

11. Randall Jarrell, "The End of the Line," *Nation* 154 (February 21, 1942), as quoted by Gottshalk, p. 231.

12. Julian Huxley, "Evolutionary Humanism," in *New Battles for New Wines*, as quoted by Thomas Munro, *Evolution in the Arts* (Cleveland: The Cleveland Museum of Art, n.d.), p.539.

13. Jacques Maritain, *Art and Scholasticism* (New York: Charles Scribner's Sons, 1946), p. 71.

14. Ibid., p. 72.

15. Munro, *Evolution in the Arts*, p. 295.

16. Iredell Jenkins, *Art and the Human Enterprise* (Cambridge, Mass.: The President and Fellows of Harvard College, 1958; reprinted 1969, Archon Books), p. 37.

17. William Knight, *The Philosophy of the Beautiful* (London: John Murray, 1898), p. 7.

18. Ibid., p. 488.

19. Ibid., p. 298.

20. Maritain, *Art and Scholasticism*, p. 21.

21. Munro, *Evolution in the Arts*, p. 488.

22. Susanne K. Langer, *Feeling and Form* (New York: Charles Scribner's Sons, 1953), p. 401.

# chapter 8

# Science, Culture Learning, and Human Community

The preceding chapters have attempted to set forth some preliminary thinking that might go into the unfolding of a more mature philosophy of culture learning. They have considered what culture learning is, why it is important, and one way that it might proceed. They have also been concerned with general principles of culture learning which, to the extent they are valid, would be applicable to the learning of any culture, historical or contemporary.

As a philosophy of culture learning, this introduction has stressed those modes of culture learning generally recognized as humanistic, that is, history, language, law, the arts, and philosophical and theological world views. In this concluding chapter we will briefly consider three final closely related matters: (1) the possibility of a scientific culture learning, (2) science as a part of culture, and (3) science and culture learning in the search for human community.

## Culture Learning as Science

The process of culture learning, like all learning, is a process of coming to know, of growing in knowledge, of passing from ignorance and lack of awareness to a state of knowing and knowing that we know. Some will prefer the more strictly psychological description of learning as the possibility of modifying behavior on the basis of remembered information in order to increase the probability of achieving preferred states of affairs. In culture learning what we seek to learn, however that term is defined or described, are the consensuses within a culture on opinion and behavior. Since all learning and coming to know, including culture learning, takes place within individual minds, whatever is learned is learned according to the abilities, capacities, motivations, purposes, and interests of the person doing the learning.

The question to be considered here is not the object of culture learning as such, that is, what is to be learned, but rather: What kind of knowledge is it that results from culture learning? Or more pointedly: Is it possible to have a scientific knowledge of the consensuses on opinion and behavior in a culture?

In understanding this question, it is important that we do not get entangled in semantics. The word *science* can be used in a number of different ways. For present purposes, however, we need to distinguish only the *strict* from the *broad* meanings of the word. Knowledge is generally considered strictly scientific only if it is governed by laws and results from investigations in such a way that any qualified investigator would arrive at the same conclusion. Knowledge is considered scientific in the broader or looser sense if it is knowledge arrived at in a systematic, rigorous, carefully controlled way so that the probabilities are high that the knowledge is accurate, valid, and authentic. The social sciences are ordinarily considered scientific in this looser sense. That culture learning, when well done, incorporates scientific knowledge in this broad sense is not in dispute.

The dispute is whether culture learning can in fact become scientific in the strict sense.

The position that culture learning aims to be a science in the strict sense is taken primarily by those scholars who refer to themselves as "cognitive anthropologists." The position is perhaps most clearly stated by Stephen A. Tyler in his introduction to *Cognitive Anthropology*. Tyler writes: "Cognitive anthropology is based on the assumption that its data are mental phenomena which can be analyzed by formal methods similar to those of mathematics and logic. Each particular culture consists of a set of logical principles which order relevant material phenomena. To the cognitive anthropologist those logical principles rather than the material phenomena are the object of investigation. For the cognitive anthropologist cultural anthropology is a formal science.''[1] Cognitive anthropology thus sets out to discover the laws that govern culture learning in such a rigorously scientific fashion that any qualified person who viewed the same data would be forced to arrive at the same conclusions.

It would be rash for anyone to say that culture learning or cognitive anthropology can never become a strict science. It is of the nature of the scientific effort and progress that new techniques, new methodologies, in fact, entire new paradigms appear on the scene and are subjected to rigorous criticism, analysis, and testing.[2] At the present stage of its thinking and development, however, cognitive anthropology seems to be based on a premise, which, if not false, is at least highly questionable. Tyler holds that ''each particular culture consists of a set of logical principles which order relevant material phenomena.'' The implication is that culture learning consists in coming to know the system of logic or the logical principles which order relevant material phenomena in a culture. The main difficulty with this position is in the rationalist reductionism that assumes a culture to be primarily if not exclusively a set of logical principles. It is in fact no more correct to say that culture consists of a set of logical principles than it is to say that an individual person consists of a set of logical principles. Both cultures and individuals use logic as a screen for motives and purposes that are nonrational or even irrational; inconsistencies, ambiguities, discontinuities, and contradictions abound.

A system of logic or a set of logical principles is one of the essential components in any culture, but it is not the whole of that culture. Further, the system of logic orders relevant material phenomena and makes it possible for the people of a culture to give meaning to these transactions and interactions in their world and to explain that world to their own satisfaction. But a culture consists of a much more complete set of *life* or *living* principles, of which logical principles are only a part. These *life principles,* which we have called *consensuses,* include feelings, purposes, motivations, affections, predispositions and prejudices, and the domains of the intuitive, imaginative, the mystical, and the creative, which are not so much illogical or nonlogical as they are translogical. The enjoyment of *haiku* poetry among the Japanese, for example, may be said to grow out of the logical principles of Japanese culture, but it also transcends them.

The cognitive anthropologists might argue that they use the term "set of logical principles" in such a broad way as to include all of what we have called "life principles." The use of the word "cognitive" seems to militate against such an interpretation, and so does the word "logical." Such imprecise use of language would be out of keeping with an effort to be strictly scientific. Life is much more than cognition and logic. Chance factors in the development of technology and the arts, the inspiration of charismatic leaders, as well as beliefs, emotions, feelings, intuitions, and intentions play a role in every culture as important as the role played by the truly cognitive and the logical. To be rigorously scientific, the cognitive anthropologists would have to demonstrate that a logical formula could be derived for representing, for example, trust, hatred, loyalty, creativeness, or love within a culture and that a further correlated formula could be derived representing the ways in which these necessarily relate to the material phenomena and the human behavior within the culture.

Whether culture learning (cognitive anthropology) can become strictly and formally scientific is an open question. Those who question that possibility are not thereby antiscientific; they simply await the demonstration and proof that the scientific method itself requires. Tyler himself reports that the cognitive anthropologists have made great strides in the study of semantic organization and formal analysis but that there still remains a vast and only partially explored territory.[3] Much more would have to be clarified, especially in the matters of causality and predictability. To say, for example, of any culture that X causes Y and only Y and always Y may be saying more than the evidence will ever be able to support. To be able to predict what changes will take place in the thinking and behavior of the people of a given culture and to be able to say with what velocity and in what direction these changes will take place might be something immensely satisfying from a scientific point of view. But whether such laws, such scientific knowledge, are possible or whether, if possible, they would be good, we cannot now say.

If it is granted that culture learning is still a long way from being a strict science, and if there is some doubt about whether it can ever attain that status, does this not leave culture learning completely in the realm of the subjective, that is, a matter of opinion, guess, conjecture, and speculation? Does this not mean, for example, that no one is ever really sure whether culture learning is valid and reliable and that there is no way of measuring the depth or accuracy of culture learning? The answer to such questions is yes, only if one holds that the knowing of anything means knowing it in a strictly scientific way. But this is not the case. There are important ways of knowing, the poetic and the theological, for example, that make no pretensions to being scientific in the strict sense. The social studies, including economics (which appears to have the highest level of quantitative sophistication among them), are scientific only in the loose or broad sense we have defined earlier. Culture learning, at least for now, can be no more scientific than those social sciences from which it draws much of its data and its methodologies.

Culture learning does not and should not, however, limit itself to what it can gain from and through the social sciences. It is interdisciplinary in the most thoroughgoing way. It seeks data and insights from all modes of learning—the scientific, the social scientific, and the humanistic. The latter have been emphasized in this introductory book because in a scientific age they are likely to be the most neglected.

Humanistic culture learning is sometimes called knowing in the intersubjective or interpersonal mode or the connatural mode. Sometimes called sympathy, empathy, sensitivity, or simply fellow feeling, this mode of knowing is based on the vivid awareness that people of other cultures are human beings, that is, persons with energies, thoughts, emotions, needs, and values that are in part at least the same as one's own, however they may be expressed. Largely intuitive, since it is a matter of direct experience rather than scientific proof, humanistic culture learning proceeds on the grounds that cultures are vastly different but that the human beings who make up these cultures have very much in common.

Culture does not exist at all except among the people who are part of that culture. And culture learning is a special relationship between the culture learner and the people of the culture that he or she seeks to learn. Unless the culture learner is capable of entering into this relationship and even willing and anxious to do so, the culture learning, if it takes place at all, will be at best abstract and sterile. In the distinction which Martin Buber makes so powerfully, the culture to be learned, grounded as it is in the people who live it, should be seen as a *Thou* rather than as an *It*. After stating that it is possible for anyone to regard a culture and its people as an *It*, Buber writes, "But the mankind of mere *It* that is imagined, postulated, and propagated by such a man has nothing in common with a living mankind where *Thou* may truly be spoken."[4]

Culture learning of the kind that involves the whole person—language, art, action, and affections as well as intellect—does not take place just in the *I* of the culture learner. Rather, it takes place between the *I* of the learner and the *Thou* of the people of another culture. Buber has pointed out that "All real living is meeting," and that "I become through my relation to the *Thou;* as I become *I,* I say *Thou.*"[5] It is equally true that all real culture learning is in the meeting with the people of culture and that I become a culture learner to the extent that I meet the *Thou* of that culture (its people) with openness, a willingness to learn, and respect. Buber goes on to say that love is responsibility of an *I* for a *Thou*. In the process of culture learning, "good people and evil, wise and foolish, beautiful and ugly, become successively real to him; that is, set free they step forth in their singleness, and confront him as *Thou.*"[6]

## Science as a Part of Culture

It might seem strange at first that an introduction to culture learning, even to humanistic culture learning, would devote only a few pages to the role played by science in the forming and shaping of a culture and to the need for understanding the consensus regarding science within a culture in the learning of that culture.

Science and the scientific way of thinking are profoundly important constitutive elements in any culture, and it could be maintained that one who does not know the status of science and technology in a culture does not really know that culture at all. Some would go so far as to maintain that the quality and scope of its science and the values placed on science by the culture provide the most telling clue about whether the culture should be classified as developing, less developed, or developed; as "status" or "contract"; as "mechanical" or "organic." These scholars see the normal path of development as passing from thinking that is mostly religious and mythological, to thinking that is mostly rational and metaphysical, to thinking that is mostly scientific and experimental. Scientific thinking is the *ne plus ultra.*

There is no intention here of minimizing the importance of science and technology in the life of every society or culture. One need only think, for example, of the impact of the harnessing of electricity and the splitting of the atom to realize the power of science to change the ways in which people think and behave. Such examples could be multiplied many times over. The relationships between science and society have, however, already been explored in a number of excellent works.[7] Culture learning that failed to take account of the consensuses about science and technology within a culture and of the attitudes of the culture toward science would be greatly distorted at best.

Nonetheless, two reasons stand out for not emphasizing science and technology as either objects of culture learning or modes of culture learning in an introduction to humanistic culture learning. The first is that science, although part of the social reality of any culture, also has a reality of its own that extends far beyond individual cultures, that is, it is not culture specific. The second is that, at least in principle, science is value free. Each of these reasons can be briefly elaborated.

Science and technology, unlike history, art, literature, theology, or law, which are rooted in particular cultures, might be considered a common possession of mankind, something quite literally in the world public domain. It is of the essence of science that everyone who is properly qualified—of whatever race, creed, sex or social condition—can become a scientist. The same is true of the applications of science in technology. This means that if the same assumptions are understood and the same procedures are followed, the results obtained will be the same everywhere. There is thus no such thing, for example, as a Chinese theory of relativity as differentiated from the same theory in Egypt, Zambia, Europe, or America. The principles and content of science, while generated by scientists who are themselves members of particular cultures, are not circumscribed by the culture in which they originated. Occasionally the attempt is made to force science to serve cultural or ideological ends, but such attempts result only in undermining or destroying the objectivity of science. As Bertrand Russell states, "Its latest manifestation is Stalin's refusal to believe that heredity can have the temerity to ignore Soviet decrees, which is like Xerxes whipping the Hellespont to teach Poseidon a lesson."[8]

This is not to say that all cultures have the same respect for science or that science does not flourish more in some cultures than in others. The sociology of science, that is, the study of the social context in which science is pursued or not pursued, will differ greatly from culture to culture. The history of science shows clearly that some cultures have greatly emphasized science in certain epochs and not in others. The amount of money, effort, and intelligence devoted to science varies greatly among the cultures of the modern world. But scientific knowledge itself can not vary from culture to culture. More specifically, one does not study physics or chemistry in China as a way of learning Chinese culture but as a way of learning physics or chemistry.

Equally important in explaining why science is not included as a major mode of culture learning is the fact that science strives to be value free. The scientist, as scientist, is interested in scientific principles or the laws of science insofar as they are true or verifiable; these principles or laws have truth value, but in themselves are indifferent to other social values. As human beings, scientists may well hope, however, that their discoveries will be of value to their fellow human beings and that any practical applications of their scientific breakthroughs will benefit, rather than retard, the advance toward a more humane civilization. Thus, for example, Galileo, whose case is so well known in all parts of the world, was trying simply to determine whether the earth revolved around the sun or vice versa. Determining that the earth did in fact revolve around the sun might challenge traditional Western ideas, behaviors, and values about man's central position in the universe. But this latter circumstance was entirely extraneous to the scientific pursuit as such.

In practice, however, even science is not as value free as scientific theory supposes it to be. Scientists cannot avoid bringing their own cultural backgrounds to their work as scientists. These cultural values are reflected, among other things, in the priorities they establish for their scientific research, in the discipline with which they pursue their science, and in the types of experiments they feel free to conduct. The scientific mentality is such, nonetheless, that it seeks to determine *what is* and *what is true* regardless of where the examinations and investigations might otherwise lead.

The culture learner is, of course, also interested in the *truth* of the culture he seeks to learn, and one of its many truths is the culture's consensuses on the nature and value of science itself. The culture learner does not at all denigrate the importance of hard or rigorous data in culture learning. But culture learning, at least in its humanistic forms, does not and cannot claim to be value free. Culture learning not only involves a study of the values of other cultures, as these are reflected in their consensuses on opinion and behavior, it also involves, as it were, an evaluation of these values. Culture learning begins with feelings of mutuality and respect and, as has been mentioned before, it includes the genuine possibility of learning *from* and not merely learning *about*. The learner and his values are part of the very process of culture learning; the culture learner engages his data personally rather than objectively. The culture learner may come in the end to reject completely the cultural values and principles of the culture he is studying, the learner might even find that a given culture functions according to consensuses on opinion and behavior that are "crimes against humanity," as in the case of Nazi Germany. But the very learning of a so-called "worst case" culture, which at first might seem only to reinforce the separateness of the *they* or the *it*, results ultimately in a deeper and expanded meaning of the *we*.

## Science and Culture Learning in the Search
## for Human Community

Science, as we have briefly indicated, in its intentions and efforts is not culture specific or culture bound. Many have therefore seen science as one of the avenues leading to the development of a viable world community. Scientific knowledge, indeed, is everywhere and for all the same; to the extent that people throughout the world share scientific knowledge, the beginnings of human community can be said to have been already made. Scientists have little trouble communicating with one another on scientific matters. The claims made for science as a liberating phenomenon are valid, and science rightly can be regarded as one of the forces or factors leading beyond culture in the direction of human community.

But the developing of the kind of full human community that is urgently needed in the modern world is not exclusively or even primarily a scientific matter. Human community, like all social reality, is in most important ways a humanistic rather than a scientific construct. Science alone can not define what human community should mean, supply its integrative principles, or specify in what ways the developing of human community should be valued or given priority. Neither can the methods or techniques of science offer guidance about the ways of achieving a community of man or of mankind. Science goes beyond cultures, but it does not yet reach to community.

The central thesis of this book is that culture learning is not only a good or a value in itself but also a way of going beyond individual cultures to the developing of an authentic human community. This assertion must be clarified a little more fully in concluding.

Lionel Trilling, one of America's most trenchant social and literary critics, states that culture learning begins, to borrow Coleridge's phrase, with "the willing suspension of disbelief." The analogy is a striking and profound one. "A willing suspension of disbelief" is an altogether different thing from a willing inclination to believe. Culture learning requires the former but not the latter. Culture learning begins with a difficult act of the will on the part of the learner. This initial and sometimes fearful act of the will sets in motion a whole concatenation of psychic changes that result in his being able to see himself, his culture, other cultures, and the community of man as a whole in entirely new ways. Trilling explains the idea more fully when he writes:

> To make a coherent life, to confront the terrors of the outer and the inner world, to establish the ritual and art, the pieties and duties which make possible the life of the group and the individual—these are culture, and to contemplate these various enterprises which constitute a culture is inevitably moving. And, indeed, without this sympathy and admiration a culture is a closed book to the student, for the scientific attitude requisite for the study of cultures is based on a very lively subjectivity. It is not merely that the student of culture must make a willing suspension of disbelief in the assumptions of culture other than his own; he must go even further and feel that the culture he has under examination is somehow justified, that it is as it should be.[9]

"A willing suspension of disbelief," once made and successfully carried through, results in a new kind of person, one who can also suspend his disbelief in the possibility of a community of man as a whole.

Trilling accepts Freud's point of view that each of us is necessarily and inevitably fully implicated in his or her own culture. Because of the depth and subtlety of the influence of the family upon the individual, culture suffuses and informs even the remotest parts of the individual mind. So pervasive and powerful is culture that the very making of the individual mind is the making of a cultural mind.

But enlarging on an idea that he sees as at least implicit in Freud, Trilling next introduces the essential link between culture learning and world community. According to Trilling:

> We set so much store by the idea of man in culture because, as I say, we set so much store (and rightly) by the idea of man in community. But the idea of man-in-culture provides, as it were, the metaphysic, the mystique, of our ideas of man-in-community. It gives us a way of speaking more profoundly about community, for talking about souls, about destiny, about the grounds and sanctions of morality; it is our way of talking about fate, free will, and immortality.[10]

Culture learning, the process by which we come to grips with the ideas of man-in-culture, provides at the very same time the bases, the grounds, the reason, the metaphysic for going beyond culture to man in his most extensive community. Culture learning brings culture itself under criticism and keeps it from being considered absolute and final. Beyond culture is humanity, human community, humankind, and any vital understanding of human brotherhood on this now village-sized planet.

The person who does not learn another culture remains largely, if not totally, unaware of the functioning of the culture principle itself and of his or her own culture biases, perspectives, and presuppositions. One's culture is simply received as given because it is largely unconscious, and because it is at least relatively satisfying it is never seriously examined. Culture learning is the release, the liberation, the breakthrough to the higher level awareness of a common humanity.

Nor should it be imagined that one can ignore culture learning and thus short-circuit the process outlined here, namely, from living in a culture, to learning another culture, to sharing in, participating in, or experiencing human community as a whole. Attempts to bypass culture learning in the search for human community may well have been the great fallacy of classical humanism, of certain of the world religions, and of certain modern economic and political ideologies. Classical humanism taught that human community is possible because all persons everywhere possess the same basic human nature. Certain of the world religions teach that human community is implicit in the fact all persons are created by the same God. Marxian Communism, as one example of modern ideology, teaches that human community is possible and will be achieved but only through the creating of a universal classless society.

All of these, however, are doomed to fall far short of providing an adequate background for the development of human community simply because they are not rooted in human experience. Such views are either based on the particularistic thinking that obtains within certain cultures or they are utopian concepts that deny to culture the power it in fact has. Culture learning, on the other hand, can be and has been experienced. The number of people, on a worldwide scale, who have engaged in culture learning has been very small indeed. But the movement is a growing one and the results are already both demonstrable and impressive.

To engage in culture learning is to become sharply aware of two equally powerful ideas:

1. That one's culture plays a central and controlling role in one's own life. Once this becomes clear, it seems so obvious that we wonder how we could have ever previously ignored it. Yet it is in the very nature of culture not to make itself apparent. Persons who have never attempted to learn another culture are likely to believe either that there are no important differences among peoples or that other people would think and behave in the same way we do if only these other people were better educated, more honest with themselves, more kindly disposed, and more civilized.

For the individual, coming to this new awareness might be compared to the sudden awakening from a deep sleep. It becomes amazingly clear that, "If my thinking and behaving are products of my culture, the same must be true of the thinking and behaving of the people of the other cultures. If other people can understand me only through understanding my culture, I can understand other people only through understanding their culture. Just as I have my good reasons for accepting and identifying with my culture, so must other people have their good reasons for accepting and identifying with theirs." The effect of such an internal dialogue can be the revolutionizing of one's whole attitude toward people of other cultures.

2. That the people of all cultures have an equal stake in the future of the planet *Earth*. This small planet has only one environment, just as it has only one sun and that environment is the heritage and possession of all mankind. Since pollution of the atmosphere and the oceans, for example, passes far beyond the geographical boundaries of any one culture or country, no one culture or country can say our immediate environment is ours to do with whatever we might. Similarly, the thrust of thermonuclear extinction hangs over the heads of all persons, all cultures, not just some of them.

Culture learning alone is not enough to guarantee the development of a genuine worldwide community of man. It is, however, a necessary first step in that direction. Culture learning is the necessary beginning of growth in that wisdom so essential for our day, namely, that the welfare and self-interest of every culture is intimately linked to the welfare and self-interest of all cultures. Founded on such wisdom, a cooperative human community might begin to emerge.

This new human community itself would have to grow cooperatively and organically. Presumably, efforts to find ways of enforcing peaceful solutions to conflicts around the world would help the spirit of community to take root. Needless to say, serious and dramatic efforts toward the much wider diffusion of economic prosperity would do the same. Much more individual initiative in cross-cultural service, work, and leisure would contribute to that spirit. The atmosphere of mutual respect and trust, rather than mutual hostility, would reduce the need for highly centralized defense and security programs and would make it possible to decentralize, democratize, and humanize all those power structures based on outmoded ideas of competing, independent cultures.

The more effective and widespread culture learning is, the better the chances for building a human community suited to the needs and desires of the people who comprise it.

NOTES

1. Stephen A. Tyler, "Introduction," in *Cognitive Anthropology*, ed. Stephen A. Tyler (New York: Holt, Rinehart & Winston, 1969), p. 14.

2. Thomas Kuhn, *The Nature of Scientific Revolutions* (Chicago: University of Chicago Press, 1962).

3. Tyler, "Introduction," p. 15.

4. Martin Buber, *I and Thou* (New York: Charles Scribner's Sons, 1958), p. 13.

5. Ibid., p. 11.

6. Ibid., p. 15.

7. The literature on science and society is vast. Two books are especially recommended; the first because it presents a general overview, the second because it reflects the thinking of one man who had a profound knowledge of

both the sciences and the humanities: *Science and Society,* ed. Norman Kaplan (New York: Arno Press, 1975), and Bertrand Russell, *The Impact of Science on Society* (New York: Columbia University Press, 1951).

8. Russell, *Impact of Science on Society,* p. 81.

9. Lionel Trilling, *Beyond Culture* (New York: The Viking Press, 1968), p. 106.

10. Ibid., p. 105.

# About the Author

JOHN E. WALSH has been a research associate with the Culture Learning Institute of the East-West Center since 1972. A former university teacher and administrator, he served as a vice president of the University of Notre Dame from 1960 to 1970. The author of *Education and Political Power* and *Intercultural Education in the Community of Man,* he has also published numerous articles on intercultural education.

Ⓧ **Production Notes**

This book was designed by Roger J. Eggers and typeset on the Unified Composing System by the design and production staff of The University Press of Hawaii.

The text and display typeface is Plantin.

Offset presswork and binding were done by Thomson-Shore, Inc. Text paper is Glatfelter P & S Offset, basis 55.